L♡VE IS WHAT IT DOES

LAURA ANN HARGROVE

TO shunda

May God bless you Richly

Keep me in your prayers.

Laura Ann Hargrove

This book is dedicated to:

The late Wallace Lee Hargrove Sr. (Pops), my father. Thank you for showing me a true father's love. I will always love and respect my father, a man of integrity and a strong provider.

Also I dedicate this book to my mother, Sarah Hargrove. I admire her strength. She taught me what true Holiness is all about. My mother is a shy woman, but her strength goes beyond imagining. Thank you Mother for most importantly introducing me to JESUS CHRIST.

Chapter One

*J*alesia Brantz, nicknamed Lea, was standing in line at Miami International Airport, waiting for her flight. She was a junior in college and was leaving college for her two-week spring break. Jalesia was so ready to get home. While standing in line, she thought about the great time she would have at home relaxing, and hanging out with her family, and friends.

Jalesia is medium brown skin complexion with a very nice shape. She wears her thick, long black hair on her shoulders. Jalesia is a Christian, and doing all she can to remain focused, while doing the work of the Lord at school, as she maintains her 4.0 Grade Point Average.

When the plane landed at Tampa International Airport, Jalesia was so excited to see Rosa, her mother, already waiting at the airport.

Rosa was forty-six years old, medium brown skin complexion, with a few moles on her cheeks. She loves her children, and make sure all of her children are well taken care of. Rosa has five other children with Jalesia being the baby girl. She confesses being saved, sanctified and filled with the Holy Ghost.

Once they arrived at the house, to Jalesia's surprise, was a silver Ford Mustang with burgundy interior, parked in the driveway. A huge smile stretched across Jalesia's face as she began clapping, praising God, and throwing her hands in the air shouting,

"Hallelujah! Thank You Jesus!"

"Mother is that for me?"

Rosa answered,

"Yes, Lea, that is for you. I wanted to tell you, but your father made me promise him that I would not tell you. Your father and I are very proud of you. You have worked hard, and you deserve this car, and a lot more. We don't want you to beg for a ride, or feel like you're obligated to anyone."

Jalesia was so excited she could barely breath. Otis, Jalesia's father, was standing on the porch with the keys dangling from his hand.

Otis was fifty-seven years old, 6'4, medium built, a light-brown skin complexion, with salt and pepper hair.

Jalesia ran up on the porch and gave Otis a great big hug and kiss. She then ran back down the stairs and gave Rosa a great big hug and kiss.

Rosa asked Jalesia with excitement,

"Do you like it?"

Jalesia was still holding her mouth in her hands as she walked around the car several times.

"Do I like it? You have got to be kidding, I love it!"

Rosa walked over and opened the door,

"As I said before, we are very proud of you. Your father and I see that you're trying to make something of yourself, and you have saved us some big bucks by you getting a full paid scholarship, so the least we could do was to buy you a car.

Jalesia hopped in the car and put on her favorite gospel CD.

"Mother, can I run across town to Marcella's house? I've got to show off my new car." Marcella is Jalesia's cousin and close friend. They are always bragging and competing with one another.

Rosa answered,

"Why don't you settle yourself first, then you can ride later?"

Jalesia was still admiring her car and said,

"I tell you what, I'll just take a spin around the block, then I'll come back and settle in, and later I will ride over to Marcella's house."

While riding around the neighborhood, Jalesia was thanking

God for how good He has been, and thanking Him for blessing her with wonderful parents. Jalesia had been riding around for about fifteen or twenty minutes, when she decided she should be obedient and go home to put away her things.

When Jalesia arrived back home, Otis had taken her luggage out of the car, and Rosa had already begun washing her clothes. When Jalesia walked through the door, Rosa had a puzzled look on her face.

"Girl, how many times must I tell you not to travel with dirty clothes?"

Jalesia slowly lifted her hands in surrender,

"I know Mother, but it cost money to wash clothes and since I knew I was coming home, why spend money when you can wash for free?"

Changing into a more serious conversation, Jalesia asked,

"Mother, is it okay if I go out tonight and tomorrow with my friends, and on Sunday I will spend all day with you?"

Rosa pulled Jalesia towards her, and kissed her on the forehead.

"Yes Lea, you can go. You have worked really hard and you need to get out, and have fun with your friends."

Rosa walked out of the washroom, and into the kitchen to start washing dishes. Smiling at Jalesia Rosa said,

"I see you have gained a little weight."

Jalesia responded with her voice filled with embarrassment,

"Mother, you are right, but the bad part about that is I don't eat as much as I did when I was home."

Rosa walked over and pats Jalesia on the cheek,

"That's because I'm not cooking for you. I know how to cook healthy and yet taste good. You're eating all that junk food, and that type of food will cause you to gain weight quick, fast, and in a hurry. Don't get me wrong the weight looks good on you. I'm sure you're having all kind of trouble keeping the men off of you."

Jalesia opened the refrigerator, picked out a strawberry soda, and sat down at the kitchen table. She continued their conversation,

"You know Mother, I do have men approaching me all the time, or sending their friend to ask me out. I don't want to get involved with anyone right now. I have gone out on dates, but the men on campus want a commitment. My education is very important to me right now. I'm focused on what I want in life."

Rosa looked at Jalesia with a smile on her face and asked,

"Lea, are you still a virgin?"

Jalesia smiling back answered,

"Of course Mother. I told you I have always wanted to give my husband a gift of a virgin wife on our honeymoon night, but you know first thing's first. I want to do a work for the Lord, get my education, get a good job, and then the husband thing."

Rosa responded,

"I know you want what ever God has planned for you."

Jalesia answered,

"God's plan is always the final plan."

Jalesia finished drinking her soda, and with an anxious look on her face, she stood up and walked towards the bathroom.

"I'm going to take a shower and get in my mustang and go over to Marcella's house. You know I want to talk a little and show off a lot."

Rosa smiled at Jalesia,

"What time should I expect you tonight?"

Jalesia answered,

"Don't wait up because it will be late. I'm going to contact Sharon, and we will probably go out tonight."

Rosa waived her index finger at Jalesia smiling,

"I thought you mentioned your walk with the Lord just moments ago, and now you're talking about going to the club."

Jalesia smiled back at Rosa,

"I did not say I was going to the club. I said I was going out."

Rosa asked,

"So what is going out?"

Jalesia shrugged her shoulder and smile at Rosa,

"O.k. Mother, you're right, I will be going to the club. I promised Sharon I would hang out with her when I got home. Don't worry, I'm almost burned out with the whole club scene. When I'm on campus, I don't do clubs, or krunk parties. Those types of parties are really wild, and I try to uphold a Christian image. I'm trying to put all of this behind me, but every now and then I hang out. I know in God's time, He will help me to do better. I try to let God aide me in what to change, because if He does, I will not have any problems on maintaining. Mother, not you, but other older people will find things to debate. We had this discussion come up in college. Take gospel music for instance. I love gospel music. Some people feel the singers have gone too far, but I can truly say, it has helped me. I like the fact that I can turn my music up and bounce to the beat, and let the base roar, and yet enjoy what they're saying. I'm not bored being a Christian, in fact, I am really enjoying myself. If people want to be bored, then they can have at it, but I don't feel they should make the young people lives miserable. We have found a way to be a Christian and have fun. Enough said, let me get dressed."

Jalesia proceeded to the bathroom to get dressed.

Rosa responded,

"We will continue that conversation later, because I want you to know how I feel about gospel music. Be careful while you're out tonight and say a prayer."

"Yes Mother."

Chapter Two

*J*alesia was in her car, driving through traffic with her gospel music blaring. She was dressed in her white shorts, gray shirt, black sunglasses, and wearing plenty attitude. The sunroof was open, and Jalesia was feeling like everyone she passed was watching her.

When Jalesia turned on the block where Marcella lived, there was a house on the corner, and she noticed a nice looking young man sitting on the porch. The young man also notice Jalesia, and he walked off the porch and called for her to stop. Jalesia slowed up, but proceeded to go. She watched the young man from her rearview mirror as he motioned for her to come back. When Jalesia pulled into Marcella's driveway, which was about seven houses from the corner. She could see the young man walking towards her. As the young man walked half way, he stood still and waved for Jalesia to come there. Jalesia hesitated for a brief moment, and proceeded to go up to Marcella's house.

Marcella met Jalesia at the door, and when they saw one another, they greeted one another with a hug, and went inside to talk. They talked about church, school, men, and some of everything. Finally Jalesia asked as she licked her lips and rubbed her hands together,

"Who is that fine brotha down the street? He is light skin, a thick-fine, cute brother."

Marcella responded as she shrugged her shoulder,

"I don't know who you're talking about, because all the young men that I see in and out of that house, are dark skinned brothers."

Jalesia stood up and put her hands on her hips,

"No Girl, this brother is definitely light skinned, and he puts the F-I-N-E, in fine. He has on a pair of green shorts and a yellow and white baseball jersey. I wanted to stop and see what he wanted, but I didn't."

Marcella shrugged her shoulder again, not the least bit interested and said,

"He must be someone visiting, but since you are interested, why not go back by there. He may still be waiting for you."

Jalesia's smile widen,

"I plan to go back that way."

Jalesia called Sharon from Marcella's phone. Sharon is Jalesia's best friend. They have been friends since elementary school. Sharon is the kind of friend that will stick with you through thick, and thin.

They made plans to go to the club that night. Marcella could not go, because she was pregnant, and Jalesia did not want her hanging out at the club.

When Jalesia left Marcella's house, she saw the young man still sitting on the porch, and he was starring down the street. Jalesia watched as he stood up and walked off the porch, and stood on the sidewalk waiting for her to come by. Jalesia drove in that direction, and when she got to the corner, she slowed down. The young man's lips spread into a wide grin as he said,

"This is very awkward but I have been waiting in that same spot, starring down the street, hoping you would come back this way. Can you pull over out of the street for just a moment, so I can talk with you?"

Jalesia responded with a shy, schoolgirl grin,

"This is awkward for me also, because I don't know you and you don't know me, but yet I stopped my car for you."

The young man continued,

"How can I get to know you? Can I give you my phone number? Or would you give me your phone number? What ever it takes, I would love to get to know you."

He extended his hand through the window and said,

"My name is Derrick Curtis Dubois, and I want to thank you for stopping. This will be some kind of story to tell our children when we get older."

Enjoying every moment and smiling, Jalesia said,

"My aren't you a slickster."

She accepted the warm handshake,

"My name is Jalesia Brantz."

Derrick's deep voice, pearly white teeth, and deep-set dimples, had Jalesia mesmerized.

"I'm not trying to be a slickster, I like what I see, and I go after what I like, and usually I get what I want."

Jalesia held her finger up to her mouth,

"Very cocky, but you're cute."

Derrick's voice was full of excitement,

"So can we get together outside of the car and talk?"

Derrick looked down at his watch,

"Maybe dinner?

Derrick paused

"Like right now?"

Jalesia looked back at Derrick smiling,

"Well actually I'm hanging out with my girlfriends tonight. I just came home from college on spring break, and my girlfriends and I have a lot of catching up to do. I'm sorry I have already made other plans. Maybe some other time."

Derrick's smile slid into a sad face and he pushed out his lips like a child does when he's pouting,

"Come on give me just a little bit of your time, and I promise I will make it worth your while. I want to talk with you so I can get to know you."

Derrick looked down at his watch again,

"Please, you have about three hours before the club starts jumping."

While Jalesia was sitting there thinking about Derrick's proposal, he walked around the car and got in on the passenger's side. Jalesia asked Derrick with a surprised voice,

"What are you doing?"

Derrick responded,

"I don't have a car with me and you do. I know this really nice black owned restaurant not too far from here that sells seafood. Do you like seafood?"

Jalesia answered,

"Yes, I like seafood and I don't know why I am doing this, but I will take you."

Jalesia asked with a tone of sarcasm,

"Do you want me to pay for dinner also?"

Derrick smiled,

"Now that is very nice of you. Sure you can buy dinner. There is nothing wrong with a woman taking a man out on a date."

With wrinkles across Jalesia's forehead and a puzzled sounding voice,

"I did not ask you out on a date, you asked me out"

Derrick answered,

"Yes, you are correct. I did ask you out, but it is so nice of you to offer to buy me dinner, and I do accept, but the next time, the date will be on me."

When Jalesia and Derrick arrived at the restaurant, the people were dressed nice in business casuals.

Derrick, being a real gentleman, came around the car and opened the door. He extended his hand to help Jalesia from the car. Jalesia had a slight frown on her face,

"I don't think we will blend in with this crowd. We have on shorts, and all the other people are dressed up."

Derrick took Jalesia by the hand and looked her up and down, then intertwined his fingers with her fingers,

"We will be alright. I know a lot of these people at this restaurant, because I come here quite often."

When they walked into the restaurant, the hostess greeted them,

"Good Evening Mr. Dubois, do you have a preference tonight where you would like to sit?"

Derrick answered,

"Yes, I would like somewhere private, nice and dim."

Jalesia's eyebrows raised and she asked,

"Mr. Dubois, huh?"

"Yes, that is my last name. Why are you looking so surprised?"

The hostess came back to seat Derrick and Jalesia, and escorted them to their table. She led them to the spot Derrick had described.

Derrick pulled the chair from the table for Jalesia, and sat across the table from her. Jalesia interlocked her hands together and said,

"You asked me, why do I look so surprised? I guess its because I have played this unusual day back in my mind, and I'm a bit confused. I am sitting, at what appears to be an expensive restaurant, with some man I know absolutely nothing about, whom I drove to the restaurant, because he does not have a car, and have agreed to buy dinner. If you look at the turn of events, that could be a little confusing."

Derrick reached across the table and laid his hand on top of Jalesia's hand,

"Well I do plan to help you with one part of your confusion, because I plan to tell you all about me, so you will not feel like you are with someone you know absolutely nothing about."

The waitress came to the table to take their drink order,

"Good Evening Mr. Dubois and Miss. My name is Melody and I will be your server for the evening. How can I start you off? Would either of you like some wine?"

Derrick extended his hand to Jalesia,

"Ladies first."

Jalesia responded,

"No, I will not be having wine, but sprite please."

Derrick was looking up at the waitress smiling,

"I would like a bottle of Dom Per ion, with two glasses, and would you please send the chef on duty to our table?"

Jalesia thought to herself,

"I can't believe I am doing this. Oh Lord, what am I getting myself into? Maybe I should tell Derrick that I'm not interested in completing this date. I can't afford these prices. I am a struggling student, what am I doing. God, please forgive me."

Jalesia looked at Derrick with a more puzzled look on her face, when she reviewed the prices on the menu,

"Can I take a look at the wine menu, so I can see how much a bottle, and not a glass, of Dom Per ion cost?"

Derrick answered smiling,

"Just get your credit card out, because you will be needing it tonight."

Jalesia closed her eyes, and massaged her temples, and Derrick reached across the table and touched her on the forehead,

"Are you alright? I hope I'm not stressing you out, because I don't want that to happen. I know the lady who owns this restaurant, so if you can't pay the tab, I will get her to pick it up."

"No, I told you I would treat tonight and being the Christian that I am, I'm a woman of my word."

Derrick's eyebrows raised and he reached across the table for Jalesia's hand.

"Christian? Wow, I did not know they make Christians so fine, and equally beautiful."

The chef arrived at the table, and he nodded his head with a greeting,

"Yes Sir, Mr. Dubois?"

Jalesia interrupted for a moment,

"Excuse me, but do you know Mr. Dubois?"

Jalesia could see Derrick out the corner of her eyes motioning to the chef to say no. The chef explained,

"I don't know him personally, but I do know of him."

Derrick cut in,

"Randy we're going to have the fried seafood platter, and don't be stingy with the portion, because I'm hungry."

Jalesia interrupted,

"I realize Mr. Dubois has ordered for the both of us, but no oysters, nor clams for me. I am not that hungry; therefore, you don't have to give me a hearty portion, and would you make mine broiled instead of fried."

The waitress came back with their drink order and Jalesia took a sip then changed her mind,

"Excuse me, I am going to keep the sprite, but I've changed my mind, I would like to order a virgin, strawberry daiquiri."

Derrick was starring across the table at Jalesia, as he took his finger and rubbed around the top of his glass, and responded to

Jalesia's drink order,

"Virgin huh?

"Yes, Virgin!"

Being the cocky man that Derrick is he lifted his finger to his lips, "Hmmmm! I'm trying to think if I want a virgin also."

Derrick and Jalesia ate dinner and talked for almost two hours, getting to know one another and to see what they had in common. When the waitress brought the check to the table it was paid in full, and she laid two angel mints on the table. Derrick reached across the table for Jalesia's hand, and he put his mint in her hand, and with a low sexy voice said,

"I want you to have my angel mint, because truly you are my angel. I've had such a wonderful evening. If you don't mind would you please take me home?"

Jalesia answered,

"I too have had a nice evening. I have really enjoyed our conversations, and we have so much in common. Since I picked you up, I will take you back home, it's in route to where I am going."

Derrick squinted his eyes slightly,

"Well actually I live out in the suburbs. I was just visiting my cousins today. I never come over this way, but after meeting you, I definitely see why I had to be over here. I know you can call this fate. God has truly blessed me today, because you have crossed my path. I sure don't want this evening to end, but I realize you promised your friends you would hang out with them tonight. Would it be possible for us to get together again, very soon? I have not been on a date like this in a long time. Meeting someone and getting to know them, and finding out you have so much in common can be exciting. I really don't want this date to end. Are you sure you have to hang out with your friends? I know this nice place I can take you to. It's not a club, but it's a social gathering that they have in my community."

Jalesia smiled at Derrick,

"I have enjoyed my self also, but whenever I make a promise, I keep my promise, because, if you don't have anything else, you have your word. This will not be the last time for us to be together. We can plan another date, so give me a call and we can schedule something."

Derrick took Jalesia by the hand, as he escorted her to her car,

"Thank you for dinner tonight. That has meant a lot to me, because women don't like to take men out."

Jalesia responded,

"I was kind of forced into it, because I don't normally take men out either. I am glad you were persistent, because if you were not, I would have missed out on a good opportunity."

Derrick opened the car door for Jalesia, and she proceeded to take him home.

Chapter Three

*J*alesia and Derrick talked so much in route to taking him home. She went through so many twist and turns that her prayer was that she could find her way back. They turned into a community called Mercedes. Jalesia had never been to this place before, and all the homes in this community looked like mansions.

"WOW! Do you really live out here?" Jalesia asked. "These houses are really nice."

Derrick dropped his head, and did not admit that he lived there, as he responded,

"My momma has a house out here, and I need to go by to pick up something before you take me home."

When Jalesia stopped at the red light, their eyes met. Derrick tried to make eye contact, but Jalesia looked away,

"Derrick, I really have enjoyed myself, being with you today. It's getting late, so I need to be going, if I am going to pick up Sharon tonight."

At the next stop sign their eyes made contact again, and Jalesia began to think to herself,

"Do I want to be alone in the club tonight. Do I want to be with Derrick at the club? No car, riding with me, and I would probably have to pay his way into the club. No, I better not. But brotha is cute, and sho nuff fine. No one will know that I'm the one paying for the date. Okay, I'm a sucker for a nice body and a cute face. I'll ask him and see what he says."

Jalesia looked at Derrick with a smile on her face,

"Derrick, do you want to go to the club with me tonight? I will pay your way since I did not have to buy dinner."

For a brief moment Derrick gave it some thought, even though he hates clubs. He then answered,

"To be honest with you Jalesia, I would love to go, so I can be with you, but I just don't do clubs. The whole club scene is not my flavor, but I will ride with you, and I can go over to my friend's house, who lives around the corner from the club."

Jalesia responded,

"No, you don't have to."

Derrick reached over and laid his hand on top of Jalesia's hand,

"I'll go with you, and hang out with my friend for a little while, and then I will come into the club and spend some time with you."

Jalesia replied,

"You can go with me, but you don't have to come inside if you don't want to. I am almost burned out with the whole club scene myself, but I promised my friend I would go out with her tonight. Again I am a woman of my word. I know I am being convicted about hanging out at the club. There is one thing I know about being a Christian, you don't have to beat anyone up with the word, because if it is something the Lord don't want you to do, He will let you know."

Derrick rode with Jalesia to Sharon's house, and when they pulled up Sharon was already dressed. Jalesia jumped out of the car and ran towards Sharon with her arms extended, and they hugged one another. Sharon was so excited to see Jalesia, and Sharon asked,

"Hey girl, what have you been doing with yourself? You are not skinny any more."

Sharon twirled Jalesia around, and checked out her shape,

"Girl, look at you! You're almost as fine as me. I know the brothas are all over you in college. With that shape you have, I know you're not the virgin you used to be. Who is the brother in the car with you? Is that the man that is knocking you up? You did not tell me you were going to bring your man. If I would have known, I would have asked Wayne to come."

Jalesia put her hand over Sharon's mouth,

"I haven't had time to tell you anything, nor answer any of your questions. You're talking a mile a minute, and no one is knocking me up. I am still a virgin. Come on I will introduce you to Derrick."

Sharon and Jalesia were walking towards the car, still hugging one another. They were so excited, because it had been a while since they have seen one another. Derrick could see them walking towards the car from the side mirror, and he stepped out of the car. Sharon whispered in Jalesia's ear,

"Girlfriend, brotha sure is fine, you shoulda brought me one of those."

Jalesia whispered back,

"They did not have but one, and since I saw him first, I thought I would keep him for my self, besides where is Wayne? I think Derrick may have a little baggage, I will tell you all about it later."

Jalesia pointed her hand from Derrick to Sharon,

"Derrick this is Sharon, my best friend in the whole wide world, and Sharon this is Derrick."

They greeted one another with a handshake.

Derrick commented in his deep voice,

"I must be Derrick no body, because I did not get an introduction like Sharon, the best friend in the whole wide world."

Jalesia took Derrick by the hand and said,

"I did not mean it like that."

Jalesia went to the trunk to get her clothes that she needed to change into,

"Derrick do you want to come in? I need a few minutes to get dressed."

Derrick answered,

"No, I will stay out here and listen to your weak stereo system. This music is really good, but your system is not producing."

Jalesia responded,

"I know, but I will be doing something about the system tomorrow. I did not have time to get it done today. There is nothing like good gospel music on a nice system."

Chapter Four

*W*hen they arrived at the club, Jalesia asked Derrick what was he going to do, and Derrick had already explained to Jalesia that he had a friend that lived around the corner.

Derrick walked up to Jalesia and whispered in her ear,

"Can I borrow your car, and go to my partner's house? I will be back in about an hour."

Jalesia gave Derrick her keys, and Derrick gave Jalesia his wallet. He had some credit cards, his driver's license, and about two hundred dollars cash, in it.

After one hour had passed, Jalesia went outside the club to see if Derrick had come back, but he was not there. When two and a half hours had passed, Jalesia went back out to see if Derrick had come back, but no Derrick. Thirty minutes later Jalesia was starting to get a little worried. Jalesia found Sharon, and the two of them left the club and walked a couple of blocks looking for Derrick, and still no Derrick.

When Jalesia and Sharon came back to the club, they paged Derrick, but still no Derrick. Jalesia was a ball of nerves now. How was she going to explain this to her mother, the first day she get her new car, and because of being irresponsible, the car is gone? It's late, and getting later, and this man is gone in her car. What is she going to do, it is now 2:00 in the morning and, she has no choice but to call her mother.

Jalesia and Sharon decide to take one last look outside, before they call home. Sharon points towards the end of the parking lot,

"Is that your car down there, it's a gray mustang?"

Jalesia looked at the car and her smile turned into a frown,

"No, that is not my vehicle, that car has tinted windows and the stereo system is basing loud, and there are five star rims on that car."

Sharon looked over at Jalesia and started smiling,

"Girl, I think that is your mystery man getting out of that car."

Jalesia's smile appeared again, as she said,

"It sure is, and I have no time for questions, nor answers, because I have to be heading home. It is past my curfew. Yes, I'm grown, but I still live at home, and what Otis and Rosa says in their house, that's the way it goes."

Jalesia was walking fast towards the car, and Derrick met her with the keys dangling from his hand. Derrick was very apologetic,

"I'm sorry it took so long, but when you told me at dinner you were going to do this to your car tomorrow, I thought it was the least I could do for you, since you took me out to dinner. I have a partner that owns an automotive shop, and I knew he would do me a favor tonight. Since your car is done, I was hoping you would spend some time with me on tomorrow." Derrick looked down at his watch, "Or should I say later on today."

With eyes and a voice of gratitude, Jalesia took the keys from Derrick's hand,

"That was very nice of you, and I would love to tell you how much I appreciate this, but I have a curfew and I'm already late, and I still have to take you and Sharon home."

Sharon interrupted as she waved her hand good-bye,

"Lea, you and Derrick can go ahead. I see my man has come up, and you know he will take me home."

Sharon and Jalesia hugged again and said their good-byes, and Jalesia walked up to Derrick and put her hand on his cheek,

"How can I say thank you?"

Derrick answered,

"You already have, and I don't need a ride home. I'll call my brother and he will come and pick me up, besides I don't want you getting into any trouble on your first day back home. I would like to see you later so I can take you out on a date, my treat."

Derrick walked up to Jalesia and gave her a big hug, and kissed her softly on the lips,

"Can we do breakfast later, because it is in the morning when you can really tell if a person's head is in the right place."

Jalesia held Derrick's hand and squeezed lightly,

"I will call you in the morning with your answer, good night."

When Jalesia got in the car, there was a gospel CD playing, and with the base going, the music was extremely nice and smooth.

Jalesia had happy thoughts of Derrick, as she was driving home,

"I really appreciate Derrick for fixing up my car, but I must pay him his money back. Oh GOD! Let Derrick be a saved man, because I could really get into a nice, polite man like him. He is also cute and fine. The kind of man you would be proud for other women to see you with him.

I wonder did I have the same impact on him, that he has on me?"

Jalesia lifted her hands in praise,

"Thank you Lord, for allowing me this opportunity to enjoy myself, on my first night back home. Lord, I love you so much for being so real in my life. Thank you Jesus."

Derrick was standing alone at the end of the parking lot, waiting for his brother to pick him up. He played this unusual day back in his mind, as he had happy thoughts of Jalesia.

"Wow, I really enjoyed my date, and Jalesia is fine and equally beautiful. I wonder did I have the same impact on Jalesia, as she has on me. I hope I did not seem cheap at dinner. Maybe the things I had done to the car, made up for me being cheap at dinner. I hope she wants to see me again. Jalesia has it going on. The fact that she is a Christian is what I admire so much. I did not want to tell her that I am a Christian. I'm not a shame of being a Christian, I just felt a little bad after I ordered the wine. She did make a comment that when the Lord wants to take things away from you, He knows how to do it. I guess since I was convicted, I need to find something else to drink. I intentionally left my wallet with Jalesia, so she has to see me again. I am going to need to be careful around Jalesia, because she is the type of woman that will get a brother in trouble, because she is definitely fine and beautiful. I can't allow myself to trip. I have been celibate, for over two years, and Jalesia is definitely the type of woman that would make you check your religion."

Chapter Five

The early morning sun peeping through Jalesia window curtains forced her out of her sleep. She heard pots and pans banging against one another. She decided to get up and head to the kitchen.

Rosa was sitting at the table preparing her famous homemade biscuits.

Jalesia walked into the kitchen and kissed Rosa on the forehead,

"Good morning Mother."

Rosa answered,

"Good morning baby! Are you going to have breakfast? By the way, what time did you get home last night?

Jalesia dropped her head,

"Sorry Mother, it had to be around 3:00 this morning, and that will not happen again. No, I will not be having breakfast. I have a date for breakfast this morning."

Rosa responded,

"I knew you would be out late last night since it was your first day back in town. You are grown now, and I respect your decisions. You know I trust you."

Jalesia kissed Rosa on the forehead,

"Thanks Mother."

Rosa inquired,

"So are you having breakfast with deep, sexy voice Derrick?"

Jalesia scratched her head in amazement,

"Yes, but how do you know?"

Rosa walked over to the cabinet and picked up an apron, she continued,

"Well he called you this morning and asked if I would remind you to bring his wallet. What are you doing with a man's wallet?"

Jalesia took a deep breath and answered,

"I was holding it for him."

Getting up quickly from the table, Jalesia headed for the bathroom without breaking a stride,

"Mother, I would love to stay and have this conversation, and eat some of your famous biscuits, but I need to get dressed in order to meet Derrick this morning."

After Jalesia showered, she dressed into a pair of jeans with a sleeveless red shirt and a pair of red sandals. She pulled her hair back into a ponytail. Jalesia picked up the phone and called Derrick. A very sexy voice answered the phone,

"Hello."

"May I speak with Mr. Dubois"?

"I recognize your voice, what's up babe?"

Jalesia answered,

"You are what's up."

"If I'm what's up, why are you not over here picking me up for breakfast?"

Jalesia answered,

"Because the date is on you today, remember?"

"Oh, that's right, I did said I would treat you today, but since I don't have a driver's license would you be so sweet and come over and pick me up? In fact, I will cook breakfast and then we can jump in my car and start our date. I know the perfect place to take you today."

"That all sound good, but I thought you told me you did not have a car."

"I said I did not have a car with me, you missed the –with me- part."

Jalesia responded,

"Okay, what ever you say. Tell me where you live and I will be right over."

Derrick gave Jalesia the directions to his house,

"I live in the same community that my Mom lives in, but instead of turning on the third street, keep going to the end, and I live in the middle house of the cul-de-sac. The only tan house on the block, 29456 Mercedes Circle."

Jalesia responded,

"Okay, I will see you in about an hour."

They said their goodbyes, and Jalesia headed over to Derrick's house.

While riding through traffic, Jalesia had her music blaring. She was bouncing to the tune of her favorite gospel artist. She remembered that she must find a way to pay Derrick back for her stereo system, tinted windows and her five star rims.

When Jalesia arrived at the address Derrick had given her, she thought to herself, "This cannot be Derrick's house." The house was huge, and looked very expensive. There was a dark green hummer sitting in the driveway. Jalesia walked towards the house slowly thinking, "This could not be Derrick's house." When she rang the doorbell, even the chime sounded expensive.

Derrick came to the door in a pair of blue jean shorts, a red & white pinstripe baseball jersey, and a blue apron over his clothes. He was looking finer than she remembered.

He answered the door with a huge smile on his face, while holding a frying pan,

"I see you made it. Come on in and make yourself completely at home. Kick off your shoes and relax your feet."

Jalesia walked in and could not believe how beautiful Derrick's house was. He had imported marble tile in the foyer. To the right of the foyer was a huge living room with white furniture and white burbor carpet. Attached to the living room was a formal dining room with all cherry wood furniture. The table was completely set with what appeared to be fine china and crystal. The gold flatware was sparkling. There was a huge picture of the Lord's Supper on the wall in the dining room. To the left of the dining room was a state of the art whirlpool stainless steel kitchen with hardwood floors.

Derrick interrupted Jalesia's thoughts,

"Hey, will you close your mouth and make yourself at home."

The house was beautiful. You could tell an interior decorator had decorated the house because everything had a place and everything was in its place.

Again Derrick broke the silence,

"Do you like omelets?"

Jalesia came back to reality,

"Yes, I love omelets."

Derrick was standing at the stove putting eggs in the skillet as he asked,

"Are you okay? I know a thousand questions are running through your head, and we have all day to answer them all. Why don't you go and wash up so we can eat."

When Jalesia came out of the bathroom, Derrick had her plate on the table in the breakfast nook across from the kitchen. Jalesia looked down at her plate and everything looked good. There were cheese omelets, grits, toast and fresh fruits. Derrick stood up and walked over towards the stove,

"Would you like some tea or coffee?"

Jalesia answered,

"No thank you, orange juice is fine for me. This food looks great! Come over so we can bless our food together."

Derrick came back toward the table and stood behind Jalesia and placed his hands on her shoulders. He slightly massaged her shoulders,

"Lighten up, everything is going to be alright. You are entirely too tense."

Jalesia blessed the food. She and Derrick began to eat and every so often Derrick would feed Jalesia fruit from across the table. It was completely quiet at the table. While they were eating, Derrick kept starring at Jalesia, but Jalesia would not make eye contact with him. Running her tongue slowly across her lips, Jalesia finally broke the silence,

"A penny for your thoughts?"

Derrick smiled back at her,

"No, you really don't want to know what I'm thinking."

"Yes, I do, or I would not have asked."

Derrick paused for a moment and with a wide grin across his

face he replied,

"I was sitting here thinking, WOW! I have never had sex in my house, and this woman sitting across from me, can make me break every rule I have committed to. Jalesia you are beautiful and equally fine. You are a woman that is not selfish, and not a gold digger. You were willing to spend your money to take me out, even though you are in college and your finances are limited. You were willing to ride me around and let me borrow your car. You are smart, witty, and not aroused by the material things that you see."

Jalesia was thinking to herself, "If only he knew how impressed I am with his house."

Derrick continued to express himself,

"You are beautiful inside and out. I told you last evening if you treat me to dinner, I would treat you from now on. You did as I asked, and now I'm indebted to you. You asked what was on my mind. Well, I was thinking I would love to make love to you like no man has ever loved you before."

Derrick was right. Jalesia did not want to really know what he was thinking. She tried to get the shocked look off her face. She swallowed hard to get the lump that was trapped in her throat to go down and further replied,

"No, Derrick. You are not indebted to me. That was something I wanted to do. I need to ask you something, but I'm afraid."

"What? Do you want me to make love to you?" Derrick asked with a big grin on his face.

"No Derrick, that is the farthest thing from my mind."

Derrick asked,

"Well, it is the nearest thing to my mind, and what's wrong with that? Do you find me attractive?

"Derrick, I do find you attractive, but having sex is not on my mind. I'm away in college, so I can't get involved with anyone right now."

Jalesia tilted her head back, and closed her eyes,

"Would you take it nice and slow with me?"

Derrick was still trying to make eye contact with Jalesia,

"So what are you saying, do you want me to make love to you, nice and slow?"

Jalesia placed both of her hands on the table. As she made eye contact with Derrick, she softly replied in a sincere voice,

"Derrick, I'm going to be up front with you. If you don't want to be with me, you can move on."

Derrick interrupted with a smirk on his face,

"No, let me guess, you like playing a waiting game, don't you?"

Shifting to a more serious conversation, Jalesia continued,

"I'm not trying to lie to you, and I would rather be up front with you. I am not playing games with you. I don't want you to expect something that I know I can't give you. I don't want to play with your feelings, and I don't want you to play with my feelings. I'm not trying to have sex. I'm a Christian, a virgin, and proud of it. I want to give my husband the best gift I could possibly give on my honeymoon night."

Derrick paused as his chin hit the floor,

"WOW!" That's fair enough. Do you want me to call the Justice Of Peace and get this over with right now? If that is a proposal to me, yes, I will marry you, even though you did not bring me a ring."

Jalesia smiled,

"Derrick, you are such a joker. I'm not asking you to marry me. I am trying to tell you that I want to complete my education before I get involved with anyone."

Derrick reached across the table and held on to Jalesia's hand,

"I know that you are honest, and I still want to make love to you, but I respect you. I am a Christian also, but not as deep as you. If you would have wanted me to make love to you, I believe I would not have been able to control myself. I am glad you were honest with me, because I had already began playing in my mind a repenter's prayer."

Derrick rose from his seat and reached for Jalesia's hand, and led her to the family room. Derrick sat on the leather sofa, while Jalesia sat on the floor next to him. He smiled down at Jalesia and asked,

"How much time do I have before you have to go back to school?"

Jalesia answered,

"I'm here for spring break, so I have two weeks from tomorrow."

Derrick snapped his finger,

"Aaah! That's not enough time for me to get you to fall in love with me."

"I know, that's why I said lets take it nice and slow."

Jalesia turned towards Derrick and pulled her knees up towards her chest. Her facial expressions changed into a more serious look,

"Derrick, whenever I share with a man that my walk with the Lord is very sincere, and that I'm a virgin, they usually ignore the part about my walk with the Lord and focus on the part that I'm a virgin."

Derrick sat up and cleared his throat,

"Jalesia, you have to understand that you are beautiful, and certainly your fine shape causes a man to react quickly. Every man wants a woman as fine as you, and especially if she's a virgin. I'm a God fearing man and certainly not as deep as you are, but my initial thought was how can I get you in bed."

Jalesia stood up and sat on the sofa,

"Derrick, I can appreciate your honesty."

Derrick held up one finger,

"Wait a minute, let me continue. I've never made love in this house, and I have lived here for three years. I have been celibate for two years. Before I became celibate, I use to play around and take women to the apartment complex that I own."

Jalesia's thought was, "This is too much information." She interrupted,

"Derrick, why are you telling me all of this? I don't think I want to know this."

Derrick continued,

"I am telling you this because I knew the first time I laid eyes on you, that you were special. I am going to do what ever it takes to win you over. My initial thought was to pull out the bankroll, and have you eating out of my hands, but you are better than that. I don't want to make a silly move, and miss my opportunity with you, so if you say lets take it nice and slow, then nice and slow is the way we go."

Jalesia crossed her legs and had a smirk on her face,

"But you don't know me. I might not be able to come up to your standards."

"My standards, huh? My standards are wherever Jalesia is."

Derrick stood up and held out his hand to help Jalesia up from the sofa. She put her hand in Derrick's hand, and stood up smiling,

"Derrick, thank you for understanding, and I hope you will not run away."

Derrick responded with a smile,

"No way, if anything, I'm running to you in full speed. Let's do something fun today. Do you like roller coaster rides?"

"Yes, I love Roller coasters, the faster, the better."

Derrick picked Jalesia up and swung her around,

"Come on lets go to Busch Gardens."

Chapter Six

*D*errick and Jalesia were in the hummer heading to Busch
Gardens. Derrick likes to play his music a little loud. He
was playing some smooth gospel tunes, and Jalesia was bobbing
her head along with Derrick. Derrick drove past Busch Gardens and
went to University Square Mall.

When Jalesia and Derrick were walking towards the mall doors,
Jalesia was walking ahead of Derrick, and Derrick walked faster to
catch up with her. Derrick took Jalesia by the hand, and intertwined
his fingers with hers,

"Would you slow down, I'm going where you're going."

Jalesia smiled at Derrick and said,

"Well actually I'm going where you're going, in fact, where are
we going?"

Derrick answered,

"I need to run into Footlockers and buy a pair of blue and white
shoes by T-Mac, and since we're at the mall, I would love to buy an
outfit and dress alike. Remember this date is on me, and I don't take
no for an answer."

Once inside of Footlockers, Derrick was modeling a pair of T-
Mac. He turned to the sales associate and asked,

"Man, what kind of shoes do you have for my lady?"

The associate responded,

"She can have the same shoe. We have them in ladies sizes also."

Jalesia shook her head no and whispered to Derrick,

"Derrick, I don't want you to spend a hundred and forty dollars on a pair of tennis shoes for me."

Derrick responded,

"You did not say no when I ordered a bottle of Dom Per ion, so please allow me to pay for this date.

Jalesia smiled,

You're right Derrick. I thank you for paying for this date, but let's get out of here because I am ready to continue my day with you at the amusement park.

Jalesia and Derrick were having fun at Busch Gardens enjoying all of the attractions. Derrick suggested they save the faster rides for later and ride the slower roller coasters first. Between the rides they would stop to see some of the shows. They were eating junk food, playing games, laughing, and tripping off one another.

After Derrick got off the ride called Kumba, he admitted that the ride was a bit much for him. Jalesia wrapped her arms around him to thank him for riding with her. She begged Derrick to ride another roller coaster called Montu with her. This ride was faster and had more twist and turns than Kumba. Derrick admitted he did not think he could handle Montu, but he let Jalesia talk him into getting on the ride.

Once Derrick exited Montu, his knees were shaking and he could barely stand on his own. Jalesia put Derrick's arm around her shoulder, and helped him to a bench. Derrick's face was red. Jalesia felt Derrick's forehead with the back of her hand,

"Are you alright?"

Derrick was slumped over on the bench and responded,

"As soon as I can catch my breath, I will be ok."

Jalesia put her arm around Derrick and smile at him,

"That ride was the bomb! Come on let's ride it again."

Derrick stood and looked at Jalesia as if she was crazy,

"I know you are out of your mind. I think I better be going home because I'm not feeling well."

Jalesia asked,

"Do you want me to drive you home?"

"No, I will be alright. I'm not that weak."

Derrick and Jalesia returned to the car and headed back to Derrick's house. Jalesia laid the passenger's seat back and enjoyed the music as they rode home.

Once they arrived at the house, Derrick fell on the sofa, and Jalesia sat on the leather chair. Derrick smiled at Jalesia and said,

"Don't get too comfortable, the date is not over. We're going to change clothes and go to the movies."

Jalesia smiled back at Derrick and blew him a kiss,

"Maybe we can do the movie another night, but I have church in the morning, so I better be getting home. I had a very good time today, and I hope we can do this again very soon."

Derrick stood up, walked over to the chair where Jalesia was sitting and knelt down in front of her. He was starring at Jalesia, trying to make eye contact,

"Jalesia, look at me."

Derrick took his index finger and thumb and placed it on Jalesia's chin. He slowly turned her face towards him,

"Look at me. What are you afraid of? Can I kiss you?"

Jalesia closed her eyes, and Derrick leaned forward and kissed her lightly on the lips.

Derrick could sense that Jalesia was not comfortable being alone with him, even though at Busch Gardens, she was hugging and pulling on him. Derrick did not force the issue. He stood up and helped Jalesia from the chair. Jalesia got her keys off the table, and reached for Derrick's hand and said,

"Derrick it's time for me to go. I really had a nice time today, and thanks for everything."

Derrick walked Jalesia to her car and opened the door. When she got into the car, Derrick leaned his head inside and kissed her on the cheek,

"Can I see you again?"

Jalesia responded,

"I certainly hope so."

All the way home Jalesia was thinking about Derrick. She thought to herself, "What a gentlemen he is, and he didn't even force himself on me." She had happy thoughts and said a little prayer,

"God, please let this be the man for me. Help me not to get over taken in the material things that I see. And Lord, please keep me so that I don't stumble with this man."

Derrick walked inside the house and leaned his back against the door and thought to himself about Jalesia. "What a lady!" He had happy thoughts and said a prayer,

"God, please let this be the woman for me. Help me to remain celibate and keep my focus on you."

Chapter Seven

*J*alesia and Rosa arrived at church for Sunday School. They were dressed similar with a light green executive suit, silver accessories, and silver shoes. The people always tell them how nice they looked when they dressed alike.

For years Rosa and Jalesia had been going to church together, but since Jalesia had been away in college, she found another sanctified church she attends when she comes home, but today she promised Rosa that she would spend the day with her.

Praise Service had begun. Rosa was standing clapping her hands and Jalesia was standing next to her playing the tambourine. The ushers were walking back and forth escorting different ones to their seat. Jalesia could feel someone's arm around her waist. It was Derrick, dressed in a dark green Arm ante' suit with a long jacket. He had on a white shirt, a silk tie, and dark green alligator shoes. Derrick's gold Rolex watch, diamond cuff links, and diamond ring was glittering and sparkling. He, by far, was the best-dressed man in the building. Jalesia slid over closer to Rosa so that Derrick could sit on the end seat.

Rosa leaned over and whispered in Jalesia's ear,

"Is that Derrick?"

Jalesia whispered back,

"Yes, that is Derrick. Isn't he cute! I didn't know he was coming to church today."

Rosa responded,

"WOW! He is a cutie and thick too. Look at those very nice deep-set dimples."

Rosa and Jalesia went back to praising the Lord. Jalesia looked out of the corner of her eyes, and saw Derrick clapping his hands and patting his feet. She knew that rolling eyes was throughout the sanctuary watching Derrick, and she had to admit, if he were not there with her, she too would be looking at him.

When the praise team started singing a slower song, Jalesia sat down and rested one hand on Derrick's thigh. She whispered in Derrick's ear,

"Good morning. I am pleasantly surprised to see you this morning. You did not tell me that you were coming to my church today."

Derrick whispered back,

"I know. I like surprising people, besides I don't have long, so I have to make the most of every opportunity, especially since you're spending the day with your mom."

Jalesia lifted up her hand,

"Thanks for coming, this is the day the Lord has made."

Derrick finished the scripture with his hands raised,

"Let us rejoice, and be glad in it."

After praise and worship service, it was offering time. Jalesia was proud to have Derrick walk behind her as she walked around the offering table. She was stopping by different church mothers, missionaries, and some friends, giving them a hug, because it had been a while since she had seen them. Derrick continued to his seat.

When Rosa and Jalesia came back to their seat, Derrick extended his arms to Rosa for a hug. Rosa hugged Derrick, and whispered,

"Nice to meet you."

Derrick whispered back,

"Nice to me you too and I'm sure Jalesia will make the introduction official later."

After the offering the choir sung two selections. Derrick was up clapping with the choir. After the choir was finished singing, the preacher got up and it seemed like the service went in slow motion. Derrick kept looking down at his watch, and shifting in his seat.

The preacher was definitely long winded.

After church was over, different ones were still coming up to Jalesia, hugging and kissing her. Every so often Jalesia would take Derrick by the hand and introduce him as her special friend.

Once outside the church, in the parking lot, Jalesia introduced Derrick to her mother. Derrick extended his hand,

"Good-afternoon Mrs. Brantz, it's a blessings to officially meet you. I have heard a lot of good things about you."

"It's a blessing to meet you too. And I have heard good things about you also."

Rosa was blushing and smiling from ear to ear and turned to Jalesia and said,

"Baby, you can go with Derrick, and we can get together later on."

Derrick interrupted,

"Mrs. Brantz, that would really be nice, but Jalesia made it clear to me that today the two of you would be spending time together. I thought that was wonderful; therefore, I called my momma and asked her if she wanted to spend time with me."

Jalesia asked,

"Derrick where are you parked?"

"I am parked about fifteen spaces down the way."

Jalesia turned to Rosa,

"Mother, give me about five minutes to walk Derrick to his car, I will be right back."

Derrick was driving his black Lincoln LS, and he opened the door on the passenger side for Jalesia. Derrick was checking out Jalesia's fine frame as she got into the car.

He took a deep breath and said,

"My, my, my, let me get you back to your mother's car before you make me hurt myself. Honey, you are too fine! You are really going to make me work extra, extra hard trying to maintain my focus. You know what you are doing, shaking your big butt all in my face. The preacher just got through talking about pulling down the strongholds."

When Derrick got into the car, Jalesia gave him a sincere look,

"Derrick, thank you so much for coming to church today. You

don't know how much this has meant to me. I will call you tomorrow to tell you how much I appreciate the things you have done. I have really enjoyed these times we've shared."

Derrick responded,

"I thank God. He has made all of this possible. Please, enjoy your time with your family because I know the importance of family. Your mother seems to be a very sweet lady. I noticed that she is a little shy."

Jalesia replied,

No Derrick, she is not a little shy. She is shy, but don't be mistaken when she is backed into a corner she will come out swinging.

Derrick reached over and placed his hand on top of Jalesia's hand,

"I better get you back to your mother, I know she is waiting. Save some time for me."

Derrick drove Jalesia back to her mother's car. When Jalesia got out of the car she walked over to the drivers side. She kissed her hand and softly placed it on Derrick's cheek.

Chapter Eight

*M*onday, Jalesia hung out with Rosa shopping at the craft stores and the Christian bookstore. All night Jalesia talked with Derrick on the phone.

Tuesday, Jalesia took her nieces to the mall and spent time with them all day. She and Derrick talked on the phone all night as they had done the previous night.

Wednesday, Jalesia spent the day around the house with Rosa, Otis Jr., and their sister, Dianiece. They sat around talking about their childhood.

Later that day Jalesia went to her church, and after church she couldn't wait to get home to call Derrick. When she called Derrick, he was not at home. She left a message on his answering machine,

"Derrick, when you hear this message give me a call. I just wanted to see if you would grace me with your presence on a date tomorrow night? Maybe we can do a movie and possibly dinner. I know the perfect place. Call me so we can set something up."

Thursday morning Derrick returned Jalesia's call. Jalesia looked at the caller ID and saw Derrick's name pop-up. She answered the phone on the third ring because she did not want Derrick to think she was anxiously waiting on his call.

"Hello."

"Hey sweetie, it's Derrick. It was late when I got in last night and I did not want to call so late. I would love to go on a date with you. How should I dress?

Jalesia answered,

"Casual, jeans and a shirt would be fine. We are going to a movie and grab something to eat."

Derrick continued as his voice rose with excitement,

"I'll go with you tonight, if you agree to allow me to take you out tomorrow. I have an awesome idea for our date tomorrow."

Jalesia replied,

"Okay, it's a date!"

Derrick asked,

"Should I come over and get you tonight?"

"No, I invited you out, and this one is on me. I will come over to your house, but once I'm there, if you want to drive, then you can."

"What time should I expect you?"

"Oh, I'll get there around five and we can decide our evening from there.

"Okay sweetheart. See you later. Bye for now."

"Bye – Bye."

Thursday night was spent going to the movies, dinner, and a very nice walk on the beach. Derrick wanted to passionately kiss Jalesia, but he wanted to be the perfect gentlemen and not spoil a perfect date.

When Jalesia arrived at Derrick's house on Friday, Derrick was excited. He had planned this date and wanted the night to be just as special as the night before.

When Jalesia came inside the house, Derrick greeted her with a kiss on the cheek.

"Good afternoon Ms. Brantz. You look beautiful!"

"Thank you, you look handsome yourself."

Derrick slowly pulled Jalesia into his arms and gave her a full body hug. He kissed her on the lips with just a little tongue.

Jalesia pulled away.

Derrick smiled at her and said,

"Pardon me for being so rude, but I have never shown you my entire house. I want to show you every inch of my house because I want you to be totally comfortable and feel free to roam. This house has five bedrooms and six bathrooms. I always said when I got grown, I would have a bathroom in every bedroom because as a child, we had one bathroom and everyone had to share it."

Derrick took Jalesia by the hand and led her throughout the house. When they stopped in each room, Derrick would give Jalesia a peck on the lips. He was getting a feel for Jalesia, to see if she was going to allow him to kiss her, or not.

Every room was completely decorated and beautiful. The patio was huge with an in ground pool and hot tub. After they toured the 5,600 square foot home, they came back to the family room.

Derrick was excited as he starred deeply into Jalesia's eyes,

"Since today is my day for entertainment, we must be leaving in order to do all the things I have planned."

Jalesia walked up to Derrick and put her arms around his waist. She put on her most seductive voice,

"Tell me, where are we going? I don't like surprises."

Derrick exclaimed,

"With the surprise I have planned, you are going to love it."

Jalesia gently kissed Derrick on the lips as she continued talking in her seductive voice,

"Tell me, where are we going?"

Derrick rolled his eyes,

"I'm not going to tell you, plus you don't have enough seducing in you to make me tell you. Come on, we better be going. We have a lot to do and a short time to do it in."

Derrick held Jalesia's hand as he led her through the huge back yard. He showed her his basketball court and tennis court. Inside the huge garage was parked a Bentley Arnage, an Aston Martin V12 Vanquish, a Lincoln LS, and a Hummer.

Derrick extended his hands towards his vehicles and asked,

"Take your pick, which vehicle would you like to ride in?"

Not trying to be the least bit interested, but thinking in her mind, "Wow! What a choice." Jalesia spoke casually,

"It does not matter to me. I will be riding and will be with you and that is what's important to me."

Derrick raised his eyebrows,

"Girl you are not normal. I thought all women like flashy things."

"I like flashy things, in it's order. I just don't get over taken with material things, even though they are nice."

Jalesia wanted desperately to ask Derrick how he had become so wealthy, but she knew if she was patient, he would eventually tell her. For now she will wait until he decides to share with her how he came about his wealth.

Derrick and Jalesia got into the Lincoln and when they arrived at the International Mall, Derrick went into the formal shop. He began trying on a tuxedo. Jalesia was standing watching him as he tried on several tuxedos. She had no ideal what Derrick's plans were for the evening. Derrick came out of the dressing room with a big smile on his face as he strutted back and forth modeling the tuxedo. He held his crouch as he turned and looked to the seamstress. With a puzzled look on his face, Derrick asked,

"I don't think these pants are fitting right in the crouch, they seem to be kind of jammed up, what do you think?"

Derrick turned to Jalesia,

"Sweetheart, what do you think? Are these pants fitting jammed up?"

Jalesia stood with her mouth held open and answered,

"They are looking a little jammed. You can definitely see your masculinity."

Derrick walked back into the dressing room. He peeped around the corner and said to Jalesia,

"You better find you something to wear, because you don't want to wear jeans where we are going tonight."

Jalesia put her hands on her hips and said with a sassy voice,

"If you would have told me we were going to a formal affair, I would have brought my evening gown that I recently purchased."

Derrick responded,

"That's why I did not tell you, because I wanted to watch and help you pick out your gown for the evening."

After Derrick finish getting fitted for his tuxedo, he sat in a chair in the women department to watch Jalesia choose her gown. The sales associate brought three different gowns for Jalesia to try on. Derrick immediately picked the champagne color gown with the back out. Jalesia tried on the gown, and when she walked from the dressing room she turned to model the dress. Derrick loved the dress, front and back. He was very impressed and said,

"That would be the one to get, you don't have to try on any more if you ask me. You are simply beautiful. If I was given the opportunity to create the perfect woman for me, to include beauty and shape, I could not have designed her better than you."

Jalesia walked over to Derrick and wiped the corners of his mouth,

"Thank you sweetie, now stop drooling."

Derrick looked down at his watch,

"If we are going to make it on time this evening at seven o'clock, we need to be leaving."

"Seven o'clock, we have five hours between now and then. I can go home take a nap, eat, get dressed, and still be able to be ready before seven o'clock."

Derrick held his index finger over Jalesia's lips,

"Ssssssssssh! Don't talk, just flow with me. Don't ask questions because I have every thing under control."

After shopping, Derrick and Jalesia left the mall, and headed to the airport. Derrick looked at Jalesia and smiled,

"I feel you over there. You want to ask questions, but trust your man. I know what I'm doing."

"My man, huh?"

"Maybe wishful thinking, but yes, your man. You told me I have two weeks to make you love me, and in a few days you will be begging me to come to Miami with you."

Jalesia's heart was skipping a beat because she knew Derrick was right. She was trying to hold it together, although she knew Derrick appears to be her dream man. Jalesia thought to herself,

"Could I be falling for Derrick already? He knows the right things to say, and he knows the right things to do. I really wanted Derrick to kiss me earlier, and I don't know why he held back. Maybe I have been too stiff. I just don't want to appear desperate. I believe he has the perfect date planned tonight, especially since we are to dress formal."

Derrick had his own thoughts going,

"I really wanted to kiss Jalesia, but I don't want to move too fast. She seems to be the perfect lady. I think after this date she will want me to kiss her.

Derrick had the perfect evening planned. He would fly Jalesia out to New York, where they would spend the evening. He had tickets to the Opera and afterwards they would have dinner at a sophisticated restaurant that he's part owner. He knew that since Jalesia was a good girl, he had to fly her back home tonight, so he already had his flight reservations.

Chapter Nine

On board Delta flight number 507, and for the first time in Jalesia's life, she sat in first class. The seats were so roomy, and the flight attendant was extremely nice. Derrick laid his head on Jalesia's shoulder. In a sleepy voice, he asked,

"Do you mind if I take a nap, I'm a little tired?"

"Of course not, but if I knew I would be on board a plane I would have brought some reading material."

Derrick ran his fingers down Jalesia's cheeks

"That's the whole idea, relax and cradle me."

They were in the air heading to JFK International Airport. Derrick started breathing heavy, which meant he was on his way to sleep.

This was all like a dream to Jalesia, everything was happening so fast. Here she was on a plane heading to New York. She thought to herself,

"Where are we going for a black tie affair? Why did we have to fly to New York for the event? What are Derrick's plans? Do I know him well enough to be alone with him in New York? Can I trust Derrick? Has he laid it all on the line? What? How? When? Why?

Derrick tossed to get more comfortable. He laid his head in Jalesia's lap and puckered his lips for a kiss. Jalesia kissed him lightly on the lips.

Derrick voice was deeper and groggy,

"Good Lord, I can feel the tension. Will you please calm down, relax, say you a prayer, and do what ever it takes for you to chill out. I want you to have a good time. You have nothing to worry about. I know that mind of yours is going a mile a minute."

Jalesia brushed away the wrinkles in Derrick's forehead,

"What are we going to New York for?"

"If you must know, I will tell you, because I don't want you to be nervous. We are going to the Opera and afterwards we're going to another restaurant that I own. Are there any more questions, or can I take these next thirty minutes to continue my nap?"

Jalesia answered,

"Get your nap, and I will wake you when we get closer to our destination."

When they arrived at the airport, in New York, Derrick had his Cadillac Seville already parked in the parking garage. Derrick drove about fifteen minutes from the airport to an apartment complex.

Derrick, being the perfect gentleman walked around to the passenger door to help Jalesia get out of the car. He put his arm around Jalesia as they walked towards the apartment. Derrick softly spoke,

"This is the apartment complex that I own. When I come to New York, I have one of the apartments for my use."

Once they walked inside the apartment, everything was in place. The apartment was beautiful. Derrick was still sleepy as he spoke,

"Sweetheart, I'm going to lay down for a few minutes. Wake me in about forty-five minutes, and I will get up and start getting dressed. Also, would you please check the messages on the answering machine and write them down for me?"

While Derrick was resting, Jalesia checked the messages. Derrick had twelve messages and all but one was in reference to business. A young lady left a message. She was begging Derrick to call her. Jalesia thought,

"I have no right to get upset nor to be jealous, because certainly this woman knew Derrick before I did."

After Jalesia played secretary, and wrote down Derrick messages she went into another bedroom to shower, hot curled her hair, and to get dressed. She wore her shoulder length hair down. She took out her contact lenses and wore her cute professional glasses.

Jalesia picked up the phone and called Rosa.

Rosa answered,

"Hello this is the Brantz residence."

"Mother, this is Lea."

Rosa looked at the number on the caller's id again and asked,

"This is who?"

"Mother, it's me, Lea."

"I heard what you said the first time but this is a New York number coming up on my caller id."

"Yes mother, you are correct and that is the nature of my call. I wanted to tell you that Derrick had a brilliant idea for our date this evening. I had no idea that he was going to fly me out to New York for us to go to the opera and a restaurant that he owns."

Rosa took a deep sigh and said,

"Lea, this is not the order of telling me where you are going. You are suppose to tell me before you leave, and not call me once you get to where you are going."

"Mother you are correct, but I'm trying to tell you that I did not know until we were at the airport."

Rosa quickly snapped,

"Do they have phones at the airport?"

Jalesia rolled her eyes, and knew if Rosa could see her she would not be rolling her eyes. She exhaled and said,

"Mother, I wanted you to know where I am, because you always told me to make sure someone knows in the event that something happens."

"Well, you are trying to now think some what intelligent. The opera last a long time, when should I expect you?"

Jalesia could see that Rosa had calmed down, and she answered with a smile,

"We have a flight scheduled for tonight, coming back to Tampa. I don't know what time I will be home but I will call you later to let you know. Of course you know it will be very late when I get in, considering our long evening and then the flight home."

Rosa asked,

"Do you trust Derrick to be in New York with him alone?"

"Yes. I do trust him. We both are Christians and I don't think he will try anything foolish."

"Well sweetheart be safe, call me and keep me updated. I do have Derrick's phone number, because it did pop up on the caller id."

"O.k. Mother, I should be going, but I will call you later. Love you, bye-bye."

"Love you too, bye-bye."

In forty-five minutes Jalesia was in Derrick's room trying to wake him. She tried calling Derrick a few times, but he did not respond, so she began to shake him, while still calling his name.

Derrick woke up with an angry look on his face. Jalesia spoke softly,

"You seem to be pretty tired. Did you want to stay in and get some rest?"

Jalesia wiped the sweat from Derrick's forehead. Derrick looked up at Jalesia and smiled,

"No, we will not be staying in. I have invested too much money on this evening to just lay in the bed and sleep. I can press through this tiredness and get rest when I get back to Florida."

Derrick got up and started getting dressed.

The Opera was very nice, and definitely different for Jalesia, but she enjoyed it. After the Opera, they went to the restaurant that Derrick owns. During dinner, Derrick explained to Jalesia that he partnered up with one of his Christian friends, and purchased the restaurant as a project. They wanted to see if the restaurant would be a success, and if so, they would open more in other major cities. The restaurant was upscale, ritzy, and very expensive. The menu was Italian, and the food was great.

After dinner Derrick and Jalesia headed straight for the airport and back to Derrick's house. Jalesia asked softly,

"Why are we rushing through the evening?"

Derrick responded,

"I thought you had to be back at a certain time. I knew I had to cram a lot in a little time. You told me the other night about your curfew, and I knew I could not ask you to spend the night in New York with me. I have no intentions on making a play for you, because I want us to have a meaningful relationship. You can now rest easy, because I know you were thinking that I would pressure you into having sex. You asked me to take it nice and slow, and that is what I plan to do. I will not pressure you. In fact, you will be asking me to make love to you, before I pressure you."

Once they got back to the house Jalesia was thinking in her mind,

"I need to go home, but I am extremely tired, and it's late. I would not want to fall asleep at the wheel and have a wreck."

Derrick and Jalesia changed clothes. Jalesia called her mom. The voice on the other end was groggy,

"Hello."

"Mother, it's me, I know it's late, and I am extremely tired. I don't want to fall asleep in route to home, so I will come home first thing in the morning."

"Baby, you are grown, and I trust the decisions that you make, but remember you are going to church with me again today. I am leaving at 9:00, going to Sunday school."

"Yes Mother, I will be there on time."

Jalesia thought again,

"Maybe I can have Derrick take me home."

When she looked, Derrick was already drifting off to sleep.

Jalesia was resting on the sofa with Derrick. He wrapped his arm around her waist. Derrick held Jalesia tighter, as he spoke with a much more deeper voice than normal,

"So, did you enjoy your date tonight?"

Jalesia answered,

"It was very nice, and yes I totally enjoyed it. I just wish we were not so rushed."

While Jalesia was talking, Derrick had drifted off to sleep.

Jalesia thought about the fact that she was spending the night with a man. How does that look from a Christian prospective? Then she remembered how busy their day was, and how tired she was. She then thought, she would rather spend the night and live another day, than to fall asleep while trying to make it home. Jalesia thought about how beautiful the date had been. She said her prayers then drifted off to sleep.

Chapter Ten

It was Sunday morning, about six a.m. when Jalesia awake to the smell of coffee brewing. Derrick had covered her with a Tampabay Buccaneer pewter and red blanket. He had placed a pair of his socks on her feet. Jalesia got up and headed to the bathroom. After she washed her face and brushed her teeth, she got dressed. She then went into the kitchen where Derrick was standing over the stove scrambling eggs.

Jalesia walked up behind Derrick and wrapped her arms around his waist, and rested her head in his back. She spoke with a soft low voice,

"Good morning Derrick."

Derrick answered with a smile in his voice,

"Good morning, would you like something for breakfast?"

"No, I might eat a little fruit, but my stomach does not feel like eggs today."

Derrick had a concern look on his face as he tried to turn around, but could not because Jalesia was still holding on to him.

"J, I'm sorry about last night, but I was so tired. Please forgive me for falling asleep on you."

"That's not a problem, but I really need to be trying to get home. I have sunday school and I will be at my mothers church again today."

Derrick responded,

"I really don't want you to go."

Derrick pulled Jalesia down on his lap as he sat at the table to eat breakfast. He continued to talk,

"This whole relationship with you and I is so unusual, the way we met and the things we do for one another. You are the first woman to ever spend the night in my house. I feel that I have known you for a long time. It is almost embarrassing how I'm feeling towards you, in such a short period of time. People would not understand how I feel."

Jalesia rested her hand on Derrick's cheek,

"Derrick thanks for your honesty because I'm feeling the same way, but I was too embarrassed to say it. We have done so much in these past few days and have spent so much time together. It is almost scary that two people can feel this way about one another so fast. Some things are not for people to understand as long as you and I understand, and then that's all that really matters. I said I would not allow this to happen knowing I will be going back to school. Long distance relationships just don't work."

Derrick responded,

"You must have heard someone say that long distance relationship does not work, because I believe our relationship can work."

Jalesia started smiling,

"I guess it would be something I have heard before, because I have never been in a long distance relationship."

Derrick had a big smile on his face and asked,

"Now, does this mean that you and I are in a relationship?"

Jalesia did not respond. She took her keys off the key holder and started for the front door. Derrick was walking behind her. When Jalesia reached for the door knob, Derrick pulled her back into his arms and gently kissed her with just enough tongue to make her want more, then Derrick said,

"You know you need to be going."

Jalesia walked up to Derrick and put her arms around his waist, then paused,

"You're right, I better be going, but I think you are trying to get into my head."

Derrick responded,

"No baby, I'm already in your head. I'm aiming for the heart."

Jalesia knew that Derrick was right, with the exception that he also was in the heart. She knew that it was time to leave, because the soft kisses were not enough.

Jalesia got in her car and headed for home. Derrick watched her pull off and he was glad that she did. He knew if Jalesia would have stayed any longer, it was going to be extremely hard for him to maintain.

Sunday service was great. Pastor Miller preached on, "God Can And God Will." After church, Rosa and Jalesia went to lunch and Jalesia shared with Rosa everything that had happened with she and Derrick.

Jalesia did not want to seem desperate, so she did not call Derrick, but he was definitely on her mind. She kept thinking about the kiss, and questioned why Derrick did not go for a deeper or longer kiss when he had the opportunity.

Monday, Rosa and Jalesia hung out at the mall and a few other stores. They were shopping, having fun, and spending time together. Monday night Derrick had not called. Jalesia was a little disappointed because she had been thinking about him all day.

Tuesday Jalesia hung out with her friend Sharon. She encouraged Sharon spiritually to get her life together. Jalesia shared with Sharon how she had moved on with her life and was now serving God completely. Jalesia talked so much until Sharon committed her life to the Lord right then and there. She led Sharon in the repenter's prayer.

When Jalesia returned home Tuesday night, Derrick still had not called. She decided it was time to break down and call Derrick, but his answering machine came on. All Jalesia could think about was when she was in New York and the message the young lady left for Derrick. She kept playing the woman's message back in her head,

"Hello Derrick, this is Rochelle, I really care about you a lot, but you won't return my phone calls. Did I offend you when I made the move on you? I'm sorry if I offended you, but I really do love you and wanted you to make love to me. Would you please call me? I don't understand why you won't return my phone calls."

Jalesia's initial thought when she heard the message was WOW!

This woman seems to be desperate. Now Jalesia was thinking,

"Why did Derrick want me to hear the message, but never asked me about it. Hmmmm! I wonder if I am just another statistic?"

It was now Wednesday morning and Derrick had not called yet. Maybe he did not get her message, or maybe he did. Was Derrick worth another phone call? Certainly he was, but she could not leave a desperate message. The answering machine came on again, and Jalesia left a soft message,

"Hi Derrick, this is J. I called you last night and you didn't return my call. When you get a chance, give me a call if you're not too busy. Hope to hear from you soon, bye."

As soon as Jalesia hung up the phone, the phone rang. It was Derrick and they made plans for the day. Derrick would be coming over in about two hours.

Chapter Eleven

*W*hen Derrick arrived, he was driving his V-12 Vanquish. He walked in and greeted Rosa. Jalesia said to Rosa,

"Mother, Derrick and I are leaving for the day. We will probably grab something to eat and just hang out."

Rosa folded her arms across her chest smiling,

"Derrick, you are such a polite gentleman."

"Thank you Mrs. Brantz. I'm sure my mother would be pleased to hear that."

Rosa asked,

"Would you two like me to cook some breakfast, and maybe sit down and talk some?"

Before Jalesia could say anything, Derrick answered,

"Mrs. Brantz, I would love to have breakfast with you. Maybe I can learn a little more about cooking."

"Come on, meet me in the kitchen, and let's get started."

When Rosa walked over and pick up an apron out of the drawer, Derrick also went into the drawer and picked out an apron.

"Derrick if you are going to help, the first thing you need to do is wash your hands."

Derrick walked towards the kitchen sink, and Rosa stopped him.

"Where are you going?"

"I was going to the sink to wash my hands."

"No, baby we don't wash our hands in the kitchen. We wash our hands in the bathroom, then we come into the kitchen."

Derrick had a puzzled look on his face and asked,

"Mrs. Brantz, I'm just curious, what is the purpose of washing your hands in the bathroom and not the kitchen?"

"First of all the Kitchen should be the most sanitized place in your house, so before coming into the kitchen with dirty hand, wash them first."

Jalesia pulled a chair from the table and sat down while she watched Rosa and Derrick prepare breakfast.

Derrick asked,

"Mother, tell me where are the pots and pans so I can assist you."

Rosa pointed to where the pots and pans were, and asked,

"Derrick, do you like biscuits?"

Derrick responded,

"I have never met anyone who could make homemade biscuits since my grandmother stopped making them years ago. It would be wonderful to have some homemade biscuits."

Derrick looked over at Jalesia and winked his eye,

"I certainly hope you can make biscuits." Derrick rubbed his stomach while smiling at Jalesia. "Because a man's got to eat."

Jalesia lifted up her eyes to comment on what Derrick had said,

"Derrick, no-one can make biscuits like mother; therefore, a mans got to eat what someone knows how to cook, furthermore…"

Rosa, looking surprised, cut in the middle of Jalesia's comment and said,

"I've been trying to teach Lea how to make biscuits, but the art is the more you try, the better you get. Lea will not take out the time to practice."

Derrick looked surprised and said,

"Lea? That name is pretty."

"Yes, Lea, we started calling her Lea, because her siblings said her name was too long. Jalesia told me that you call her J. Believe it or not, her cousins also call her J."

Derrick pulled a chair from the table while Rosa rolled out the biscuits. She told him all about Jalesia's childhood.

Derrick commented on what Rosa had been saying,

"I'm learning more and more about Jalesia in one day than I've learned in all of our conversations together. One of the best things I have learned that she knows how to cook."

Jalesia was smiling and nodding to Derrick's comment,

"Yes, I know how to cook, but so do you, which is even better."

Rosa looked at Derrick with a serious look and said,

"This situation is so unusual. Derrick, it feels almost like we've known you for some time. I have never felt this comfortable with anyone I just met."

Derrick responded,

"Mother, I feel the same way. The first time I saw Jalesia I was determined that day, I was going to wait until she came back by. I believe that meeting Jalesia was orchestrated by the Lord. I asked Him for exactly what I wanted, and so far it looks like God has answered my prayers."

Rosa started humming while she was rolling the biscuits in her hands.

Smiling at Derrick, Jalesia told him,

"This is the special ingredient to the biscuit that I haven't learned, because whenever mother starts humming, those biscuits take their form."

While Rosa and Derrick were busy cooking breakfast, Jalesia started preparing the table. When everything was ready, they sat at the table together for breakfast. They had hot, homemade biscuits, bacon, eggs, grits, sausage, and orange juice. The syrup was on the table, just in case someone wanted syrup with their biscuit.

While sitting at the table, they all joined hands and Rosa nodded toward Derrick so he would bless the food.

Derrick began to pray in his deep sincere voice,

"Most gracious Father, we thank you for this food that has been prepared, and the hands that prepared the meal. We thank you for making a way to purchase this food. Sanctify this food that it may be nourishment to our bodies and strengthen our souls with the bread of life. In Jesus' name. Amen."

"Amen."

Derrick had a sad look on his face as he softly spoke,

"Times like this makes me miss my dad. I was never given a chance to know him, and now he is gone to be with the Lord. I have vowed that if I ever have children, I would have an awesome relationship with them, because I knew what it was like not having a father around."

Rosa reached over and gently placed her hand on top of Derrick's hand.

"Oh! I'm sorry to hear that about your father, but I can tell you are going to be a wonderful father."

A tear fell from Derrick's eye. Jalesia did not want him to feel uneasy, so she changed the subject.

"If you want your biscuit to taste really good, try eating one with a little syrup."

They all talked and laughed while eating breakfast.

After breakfast Derrick and Jalesia cleared the table and washed the dishes. Rosa left out of the kitchen and went into the laundry room to start her chores.

Derrick looked at Jalesia and asked,

"So, what's on the agenda for us today, tomorrow, Friday and Saturday?"

Jalesia put her hands on her hips and waved her index finger in the air,

"What make you think you can book my schedule for the rest of the week?

Derrick's grin widen,

"Because I got it like that. I left the early part of the week for you to hang out with your family and friends."

Derrick stood up from the table and extended his hand to help Jalesia up and said,

"Let's go do something fun. I want to spend some private, quality time with you before you leave.

Jalesia answered,

"I would love to do something fun. What did you have in mind?"

Derrick held his index finger up to his lips,

"Let me see if I can try this again. Just flow with your man, I have some things in mind. I'm sure you will enjoy it."

Jalesia's smile widen,

"My man huh? That is starting to sound really nice."

Derrick quickly responded,

"Does that mean we're in a relationship now."

Jalesia answered,

"I did not say that. I was thinking about how nice 'my man' sounded."

Derrick commented,

"Take your time. I want everything with you to be right."

Chapter Twelve

*D*errick and Jalesia went to the mall. They were walking hand in hand. Derrick was smiling at Jalesia and asked,

"Are you going to answer my question about you and I in a relationship? I have not forgotten that you have not answered me yet. I remember the first day I met you, you told me that you did not want to get involved with anyone, because of the goals you wanted to accomplish. I will not interfere with your goals. I just want to be a part of the goals. Once you have accomplished what you want to do, then you and I can move forward."

"Derrick, we will definitely discuss that before I leave going back to Miami, but right now is not a good time to discuss that."

Derrick dropped his shoulders and said,

"Well that sounds like a No to me."

"It is not a No, it's just something I think we need to discuss later. Let me ask you a question, since we have not discussed it. Who is Rochelle?"

Derrick put his arm around Jalesia's shoulder and pulled her closer to him and said,

"Oh, now I get it. It is not what you think. Rochelle is this girl my business partner tried to set me up with. I went on two dates with her and she fell in love. I explained to her that I did not want to see her any more, but she continues to call. I ignore her calls, nothing more, nothing less. End of story."

Derrick and Jalesia had spent the entire day together. While at the mall, Jalesia went to the barbershop with Derrick and Derrick went to the nail salon with her. The two of them were having fun together. Derrick went into the men shoe store, while Jalesia stopped into Victoria's Secret to purchase some body lotion. While inside of Victoria Secret, a young man approached Jalesia,

"Jalesia Brantz?"

"Vincent Curry?"

Vincent walked over and hugged Jalesia and said,

"Jalesia, how have you been doing?"

"I've been doing fine. I'm currently attending college at the University of Miami and I'm home for spring break."

Vincent was not a stranger to Jalesia. They have known one another from Junior High School. Vincent twirled Jalesia around as he checked out her body,

"My, my, my! What have you been doing with yourself? I can't talk about how skinny you used to be, because no one would believe me as fine as you are now. Do you have a man, or are you free to roam?"

"No, I'm not free to roam. I am seeing someone, in fact my boyfriend is somewhere in the mall."

Vincent shook his head at Jalesia and said,

"You are still trying to play hard to get. I know you are here alone. You just don't want to go out with me. I'm going to follow you around until I see this mystery man because I don't believe you."

By this time Derrick was walking up, and when he saw Jalesia talking to the gentleman, he took a seat on the bench outside of the store. Derrick could see that Jalesia and the gentleman was having a good time because Vincent would smell the lotion on Jalesia's hand, or she would smell the lotion on his hand. They were laughing and talking about who knows what. Derrick started to feel his pressure rise just a little, and then he thought,

"I can't get angry because Jalesia is beautiful, and men are going to approach her, especially when they don't see her with someone else. Besides, Jalesia is afraid to commit to me anyways."

Derrick continued to watch them smelling different scents and candles. The gentleman would take Jalesia's hand and rub it between his hands. Jalesia started looking at some of the lingerie, and the gentleman was still following her. Derrick decided that it's time for him to make his presence known. He did not want this gentleman watching Jalesia buy underwear.

He stood up and walked into the store.

When Jalesia saw Derrick, her eyes lit up, and she put her arm around Derrick's waist and said,

"Sweetheart, what took you so long? I was just telling Vincent about you. Vincent and I went to Junior High School together, and I told him I was in the mall with my boyfriend, but he did not believe me."

Derrick slipped his arm around Jalesia's waist and kissed her on the cheek and said,

"Well Sweetie, I am definitely here."

Derrick turned to Vincent with his hand extended,

"My name is Derrick."

The smile disappeared from Vincent's face as he shook Derrick's hand, and said his farewells to Jalesia.

Derrick turned to Jalesia with a big smile on his face, and said

"I heard you call me your boyfriend. I hope you meant what you said. By the way, I bought something for you."

Jalesia asked,

"What is it?"

"I'm not telling you. I will give it to you later."

"Why not give it to me now? You know how I am about surprises."

Derrick waved his index finger at Jalesia,

"I am not going to tell you because I want to give it to you when the time is right."

Chapter Thirteen

*D*errick opened the passenger door for Jalesia, and once she got inside, he starred into her eyes,

"Why is it that you never make eye contact with me?"

"I do make eye contact with you, just not as often as you try to."

Derrick reached inside the bag he was holding and pulled out some flavored chap sticks.

Extending the chap sticks towards Jalesia, Derrick asked,

"Which flavor do you like?"

Jalesia picked out the strawberry flavor. She smiled at Derrick and said,

"I think I would like this one."

Derrick took the chap sticks from Jalesia's hand and rubbed some on his lips. He then leaned inside of the car and kissed Jalesia softly on the lips, and asked,

"So what do you think?"

Jalesia licked her lips and said,

"I don't know what I think."

Derrick put some more chap sticks on, and kissed Jalesia softly again, this time brushing his tongue on her lips. He then reached into his pocket and gave Jalesia a long, skinny, gold box and whispered,

"This is a little something I picked up for you while you were in Victoria's Secret flirting with Vincent."

Jalesia responded,

"Am I sensing a little bit of jealousy?"

"No, how can I be jealous? I expect men to approach you and I like the way you handled yourself today."

Jalesia opened the box, and inside was a diamond cross on a 21 inch platinum necklace.

Jalesia held her hand over her mouth,

"Derrick, I can not accept this. You must have paid a fortune for this necklace."

Derrick was a little more serious as he said,

"Why is it that everything I purchase for you, you have a problem accepting it from me?"

Jalesia answered,

"Because you don't give me little things like a book, flowers, or something inexpensive, you give huge gifts and I'm not used to receiving gifts of this value. People don't get gifts like this when they have been married for years."

Derrick shrugged his shoulders,

"If I can afford it, what is wrong with that? Would you please turn around so I can put the necklace on you?"

After Derrick put the necklace on Jalesia, he got in on the driver side, and proceeded to leave the mall. At every stop sign and red light Derrick would look over at Jalesia, trying to make eye contact. She had her head down admiring her cross.

When Derrick arrived at Jalesia's house, he explained to her that he had to take an urgent business trip to New York. Derrick explained that he would not be able to see her on tomorrow, but wanted to spend Friday evening with her when he returned.

Jalesia was disappointed and explained to Derrick that she would be leaving on Sunday going back to school.

Derrick leaned over and gently kissed Jalesia. He then walked around to the passenger side and helped her out of the car. Derrick looked deep into Jalesia's eyes,

"Jalesia, please understand what I do for you there are no strings attached. You make a person want to do more because you don't expect a lot."

Derrick walked Jalesia to the door and Jalesia kissed Derrick on the cheek.

"Have a safe trip to New York and I will see you on Friday."

Derrick started down the stairs and turned back around,

"You still have not told me if I am your man or not. I need to know, so when I go to New York tomorrow, I can brag about my lady. Everyone has tried to set me up with other women and I think they don't believe there is a woman out there for me. I'm so glad I waited because I would have missed an opportunity to be with you."

Jalesia wrapped her arms around Derrick's neck. She kissed him lightly and she said with a smile,

"Yes Derrick, we will try a relationship, but if you feel the distance is too much, then let me know and I will do the same."

Derrick picked Jalesia up and twirled her around and said,

"Sweetheart, I don't foresee having any problems with a distant relationship. I know that at any time I want to see you, I can get on board a plane and get to where you are."

Jalesia had a sincere look on her face and said,

"God is good. It's almost impossible to have a man now days, that is not pressuring a woman into having sex. I don't know what to say about you. I know what I asked God for and He has answered my prayers."

Derrick took Jalesia by the hand and looked deeply into her eyes and said,

"I am committed to the Lord and I have to maintain my focus. I have no intentions of pressuring you. Understand that in this day we're living in, women are just as bad about pressuring men into having sex. I too asked God for specifics and He has also answered my prayers. I plan to do whatever it takes to make this relationship work. I have never had a woman as special as you."

Derrick starred deeply into Jalesia's eyes and she starred back. Jalesia wanted desperately for Derrick to kiss her but he did not. She squeezed Derrick's hand,

"I guess I better get in the house because Otis does not like courtship on the porch."

Derrick pulled Jalesia into his arms and gave her a hot passionate kiss. Jalesia closed her eyes and at that very moment she was on cloud nine. He then leaned forward and kissed her softly on the forehead. Derrick smiled softly,

"Think about me while I'm gone."

Derrick strutted off the porch and tossed his keys in the air. He got back into his car, blew the horn at Jalesia, and sped away with excitement.

Jalesia stood on the porch and wrapped her arms around herself and thought,

"Oh God! How can I feel like I do about this man in this short period of time? Derrick is a fine young man. I was always taught if you wait on the Lord, He would come through for you. Boy! He came through in a big way for me. Thank you Jesus!"

Derrick was driving through traffic with his music blaring. He was feeling good that he finally got an answer from Jalesia. He couldn't wait to tell everyone about his girlfriend.

Derrick thought to himself,

"Thank you Jesus! This is exactly what I've always wanted, a fine, beautiful, Christian woman. Wow God! You sure know how to deliver. I will be forever grateful. Help me to treat Jalesia like she deserves to be treated. She will be my queen and I will treat her like a queen. Thank you Jesus!"

Chapter Fourteen

*F*riday night had finally come. When Jalesia arrived at Derrick's house, she went into the trunk to get the gift that she had purchased for him. He was watching Jalesia from the window waiting for her to walk through the doors. Derrick was casually dressed when he answered the door. He was wearing a black mesh shirt and a pair of loose fitting jeans. Derrick was looking as fine as usual with his muscular physique showing through his shirt.

As soon as Derrick opened the door and Jalesia walked in, he pulled her into his arms and kissed her. This kiss did not leave Jalesia wanting more because she got it all the first time. When Jalesia's lips were finally free to speak,

"WOW! Good-evening to you too."

Derrick looked at Jalesia with a smile on his face,

"You have been on my mind all day and I've watched you from the window taking your time getting out of the car. I could not help but to notice how beautiful and sexy you are. I could not wait for you to get in here. While I was in New York, I could not get you off my mind."

Derrick pulled Jalesia in his arms again for another passionate kiss, and this time she could feel his body pressing ever so closely to hers. Slowly lifting up her eyes, she looked romantically into Derrick's sexy eyes,

"Maybe we should find something else to do because how my

body is feeling, you are going to make me get in trouble."

Trying to change the flow of the evening, Jalesia lifted the gift bag that she had in her hands. She backed away from the door while Derrick locked the door behind them. Jalesia walked towards the family room as Derrick followed closely behind her. Derrick took her by the hand and pulled her into his arms again.

Derrick responded in a low sexy voice,

"Maybe our bodies are feeling the same way. I have not felt this way in a long time. I want to make love to you."

Jalesia responded as she starred back into Derrick's eyes,

"This is the first time I have ever felt this way before. I know I've said all my life that I wanted to wait until I'm married, but I want you to make love to me."

Jalesia wrapped Derrick in her arms, and initiated the next kiss. Her body desired Derrick and she did not want to fool him nor did she want to fool herself any longer. When she felt the motioning of Derrick's body against hers, she knew this feeling was a different feeling than she had ever felt before. She whispered in Derrick's ear,

"Derrick, I do want you to make love to me. I want you to love me the way you think I want to be loved. Teach me how you want me to love you."

Derrick led Jalesia into the master bedroom.

They were standing at the foot of the bed and Derrick knew Jalesia wanted him as much as he wanted her. He held Jalesia in his arms, as she gently rubbed her hands down the tightness of his back.

Their lips were once again meeting as their passion deepened.

Derrick unbuttoned Jalesia's blouse and unzipped her skirt. After he slowly removed her clothing, with the exception of her bra and panties, he kissed her passionately. Derrick's breathing became more rapid. Moans from inside him matched Jalesia's. Jalesia stood before Derrick in her bra and panties and thought to herself,

"This is going against everything I have told others. Is it too late for me to stop now? A part of me really wants to do this, and the other part knows that this is wrong. I can't do this. I will be letting God down. Oh God! I need your help."

Derrick continued to kiss Jalesia. He kissed her tenderly on the forehead, the tip of her nose and her cheeks. His tongue grazed her lips. Derrick unzipped and stepped out of his pants. He proceeded by pulling his shirt over his head and exposing his ripped, tight, muscular upper body. He stood before Jalesia in his fitted silk briefs and thought to him self,

"This is wrong. I will be going against everything I said I would not do. I feel if I make love to Jalesia she will not want any one else. I will have her eating out of the palm of my hands. Oh God! Help me. I know that I'm about to do something that is completely wrong. But God, it feels so good right now. I need your help."

When Derrick wrapped Jalesia in his arms this time, she could feel his hard massive body pressing against hers. The kiss was now gentle and Jalesia was lost in her own urges. She had allowed herself to drift in her desires. It wasn't until Derrick laid her on the bed and unfastened her bra that she came rushing back to reality. Jalesia thought again,

"God have I gone too far to stop? I really want Derrick to make love to me. I know this is wrong. This is really wrong and I want to stop, but I can't. Oh God! What can I do? Help me Lord.

Jalesia called Derrick's name softly,

"Derrick, I don't think I can do this."

Derrick stopped for a moment and looked into Jalesia's eyes and said,

"I love you and I really want to make love to you. I promised you I would never force you to do anything. I want you to want me as much as I want you."

Derrick moved in again, passionately kissing Jalesia. Jalesia held on tighter and said,

"Derrick we have to stop." But on the inside she was wanting more and more of him.

He removed one bra strap at a time, and affectionately kissed her on the shoulders. He spread her legs and put his body weight on her. Derrick looked down at Jalesia and the tears fell from her eyes, as she spoke softly,

"Derrick, I do love you and I want you to make love to me."

Jalesia was holding on to Derrick tightly. The tears moved Derrick deeply and suddenly Derrick stopped. Jalesia asked,

"Derrick, what is wrong? Do you want me?"

Derrick closed his eyes and took a deep breath,

"This is what's wrong, the fact that I do want you but I can't have you."

Jalesia looked up at Derrick as he wiped her tears away, and Jalesia said,

Derrick, you are a special man to me. You said you would make me love you in two weeks, and you have succeeded."

Derrick sat up on the side of the bed. He leaned over and kissed Jalesia softly. His voice was low and sexy,

"Honey, I did want to make love to you, but we did the right thing. You said you wanted to wait until you are married and that's the right thing to do. I want your first time to be special, just like you want and deserve. I promise the first time will be so special you will never forget it."

Derrick got up and went into the bathroom and took a shower. While Derrick was getting himself together, Jalesia went into the other bathroom to get herself together.

After Jalesia finished getting dressed, she went into the family room and was sitting on the sofa with a look of embarrassment on her face when Derrick came into the room. He spoke softly,

"Sweetheart, don't feel embarrassed with me, because if anyone should be embarrassed, it should be me. I was the one getting all hard and hot up in there. I had to take a shower just to cool down some. I think what happened here tonight will help us in the future. When we feel the desire like we felt, we need to find something else to do."

Jalesia was still feeling a little embarrassed.

Derrick responded,

"I have an idea, lets make homemade ice cream and sit out on the patio and watch movies."

Jalesia responded,

"That sounds like an excellent idea to me."

After they made homemade ice cream, Derrick laid stretched out on the chaise and Jalesia laid in front of him as she leaned back in his arms and watched movies.

Jalesia turned to Derrick with a sincere look on her face,

"Derrick, do you remember when you told me if I ever have any questions to just ask and you would answer?"

"Yes I do, so go ahead and ask me."

"I want to know how can a young man like yourself be so successful and wealthy?"

Derrick sat up,

"I was waiting for you to ask me and I only tell this to people I know is genuinely interested. My father was a doctor and he was accidentally killed. He was a wealthy man. He owned the apartments in New York and in Florida. I was my father's only child. My stepmother could not have children.

My mother was a poor black woman living in the projects with two other children. My father would pay my mother not to tell anyone that I was his son. He did not want to damage his reputation.

After my father's death, the royalties were shared between my stepmother and me. My father left a will and a recorded message for me. If anything were to happen to him, everything he owned would go to me. My stepmother and I would share the 3.75 million dollar insurance policy.

The tape that my father left was very painful. He apologized for not being able to admit I was his only child." Derrick started crying and Jalesia wrapped him in her arms.

"My father shared with me the only reason I was always in the doctor's office was because that was his only opportunity to hold me, to rub my head, and kiss me.

For many years I never knew why I had to go to the doctor so many times during the year, and my siblings never went. For years I thought I had something wrong with me, and my mother did not want to tell me. Every time we would run into a financial struggle, my momma would always take me to the doctor."

Jalesia wiped the tears from Derrick's eyes as the tears began falling from her own eyes. She held him close and said,

"Everything is ok, you can share this with me."

Derrick continued,

"The will my father left stated, if anything happened to him, everything would be paid for. I inherited all the cars, the doctor's office, and the apartments in New York and in Florida. The doctor's office was the only thing that I sold. The two apartment complexes keep me busy. I bought the seafood restaurant in Tampa for my momma, so she could have something to do. The restaurant in New York was a business adventure. My partner and I decided if it were a successful adventure, we would open more in other major cities. I decided to wait for now because I don't want to get burned out running back and forth.

Here I am today, a Twenty-seven year old successful, black, Christian man, waiting on my lady to finish college. I look forward to marrying her so I can finally make love to her. But I am willing to wait.

Chapter Fifteen

It has been almost six months. Jalesia was on her way home for winter break. Derrick had not visited her at all. They talked every day, whether it was short conversations or long conversations. Jalesia had been a bit surprised that Derrick had not visited. Before she left, Derrick was telling her how she was going to get tired of looking at him.

When Jalesia arrived home Thursday night, she did not want to seem like she had been missing Derrick, even though she did. Jalesia did not go to see Derrick, but she did call him on the phone to let him know she was home. They made plans to see one another the next day.

After Derrick hung up the phone with Jalesia, he called his sister, Paula, in Texas. Paula is the kind of person that tells it like it is. She does not sugarcoat things, nor does she spare your feelings. So if you are a sensitive person, don't ask Paula.

Derrick was a little troubled and wanted to talk to a woman. He did not want his mother to know he was troubled; therefore he called Paula. The phone rang, and Paula answered,

"Hello?"

"Paula, this is D."

"Oh-oh, what's wrong?"

"Paula there is nothing wrong. I just need to talk with you."

Paula chuckled slightly,

"Sounds like woman trouble to me."

"I guess you can say that. I met this girl, and I have really fallen for her. I don't want her to know how much I am into her, because she may think I am crazy."

Paula rolled her eyes up and sucked her teeth,

"Derrick, not you, the man who always say he does not care what people think, but go ahead and finish your story."

Derrick continued,

"Okay, I met this girl and her name is Jalesia. She could be the one. I really admire her a lot. We have known one another for six and a half months and I really care about her. I have never had sex with her; therefore it is not a physical thing. When I met her she took me out to dinner and let me borrowed her car. She never knew I had money so I know she is not after my money."

Paula interrupted,

"Derrick, don't tell me the extra long version, kinda get to the point."

Derrick commented,

"Stop being so rude and let me explain. I don't want to pour out my heart to her, because I don't want her to run away. I don't think our relationship has been long enough for me to feel the way I do. I could see myself marrying this girl, once she has completed college. She thought I would be visiting her a lot while she was away in school, but I have not interrupted her studies. I want her to remain focus and not have to worry about her boyfriend interrupting. I'm confused. I don't know what I should do. I talked to her mother, but I need to hear from someone in my family. Deep down inside, I really do love her but I just can't express my love to her."

Paula responded,

"WOW! I can finally speak. I have a few questions I need to ask you. Are you concerned about what people will say? Or, are you concerned that Jalesia may not feel the same way about you?"

Derrick answered,

"I think a part of me is concerned about what people will say. I feel that it has not been enough time since we met for me to feel the way I do. I really, really, really want to marry her. She tells me all the time how much she loves me, but I have not told her that I love her, even though I really do."

Paula started laughing,

"Okay, I should call you Kendall Junior." Kendall is Paula's husband. "Kendall told me that he was the same way, afraid to tell me that he loved me because he did not want to run me away. He thought people would think he was crazy. But you don't love people, you love Jalesia, and as long as she knows it, that's all that matters. If she is telling you that she loves you, then she does. Don't let people make you miss out. You are already established, you know what you want, and you can go for it.

Paula paused for a moment, then continued,

"Jalesia must be pretty special. I have never heard you say you would marry anyone. I thought the only marriage I would ever see you in, would be when Jesus comes back. My suggestion to you would be to go after her. If she is that special, then there is someone else out there who would want her as much as you. Someone, who would not be afraid to tell her that he loves her. When we are pouring out our heart to a man, and he never express himself, it begins to get old. If she is worth going after, I say go for it. And D, I will see you at the wedding...."

Derrick's voice began to tremble,

"Paula, I want to say thank you. I want Jalesia in my life, and I will do what ever it takes to get her. I am not afraid to tell her that I love her. I will tell her as well as show her, because she is just that special. She is also a Christian. You said she must be pretty special, and she is. I know what I need to do now, and I will do what ever it takes to win her over. Thanks Sis, I love you."

"Love you too, good-night."

"Good night."

Chapter Sixteen

Rosa answered the door. It was a florist standing at the door with a dozen of yellow roses addressed to Rosa and a dozen of red roses addressed to Jalesia. Rosa placed the roses on the table in the living room. Then, she proceeded into the kitchen to complete breakfast.

While breakfast was cooking, Rosa was playing her gospel CD. It was Friday morning. Rosa's baby was home, and she was feeling really good. The smell of breakfast cooking caused Jalesia to wake up. She then washed up, got dressed, and came into the kitchen with Rosa.

Jalesia walked into the kitchen, hugged Rosa and said,

"Good-morning Mother, we need to talk. I need to bring you up to date on Mr. Derrick Dubois."

"Is everything alright? Our roses that Derrick sent are on the table."

Jalesia answered,

"Yes Mother, every thing is alright, but I want to talk to you about some unusual feelings I'm having in my body."

Rosa pointed towards the chair,

"Sit down baby and tell me what's on your mind."

"I have been committed to Derrick, and I believe I love him. In fact, I know I love him. Whenever I am with him, I get these sexual desires for him. I have never had sex with Derrick, or any other man. In talking with my girlfriends, they always tell me you can't miss what you've never had. But Mother, I do have desires for Derrick."

Rosa spoke as she had a puzzled look on her face,

"Well, it's obvious, that your girlfriends don't know what they are talking about. If you are hugging, kissing, holding, or being held, then your body will desire more and more. Before you know it, you are desiring sexual pleasures."

"But Mother, I don't want to stop all affection with Derrick, and I also don't want to disappoint God. My walk with the Lord is getting deeper, and for no one would I jeopardize my walk with God."

Rosa reached for Jalesia's hand,

"Baby, you have your choices to make and you must do what you know is right to do. Pray and ask God to lead you. If Derrick loves you, he will wait for you and not pressure you."

"Mother, it's not Derrick. He has been able to hold out and put himself under subjection. It's me! I am the one that asked him to make love to me, and he would not. I was totally embarrassed."

Rosa put her hand up to her mouth,

"Oh my God!! I know you felt embarrassed."

Jalesia answered as she held her head down in shame,

"I believe that's when I knew I loved Derrick. He respected me enough not to disrupt my life. The only thing I have a problem with, I tell Derrick all the time that I love him, but he never tells me that he loves me."

Rosa was still looking at Jalesia with a surprised look on her face.

"He loves you, but men are afraid to express their love. Be patient, after while he will express himself. It is one man in a million that would be asked by a virgin to make love to her, and he turns her down. That man loves you, and he is willing to wait for you."

Jalesia shook her head in agreement,

"I know he loves me and I know he is willing to wait until I finish school, but I want to hear it from him. I think it's this long distant relationship. Maybe I should break up with him until I finish school."

Rosa put her hands on Jalesia cheeks and said,

"Before you start thinking like that, just hold off. Please don't tell Derrick that I told you this, but I don't want you to do anything silly. Derrick came by the house to talk with me while your were away. He shared with me how much he loves you. The man really loves and respects you, but he doesn't know how to handle you. I shared some motherly advice with Derrick, and I think you will see a different man. Remember what I told you, Derrick does love you."

Jalesia kissed Rosa on the cheek,

"Thanks Mother for looking out for me. I was just about to do something silly. I was going to break up with Derrick with the hopes that he would want me back. I guess if we can be honest with one another, we will not have to play these silly games to keep a healthy relationship."

Rosa responded,

Lea, always remember before you ever make any haste decisions always pray about it and ask God. Keep that in mind for this time and in the future. You said that your walk with the Lord has deepened, now you have to trust Him more with every aspect of your life."

Jalesia concluded,

"Thanks Mother, I thank God for you. You are always looking out for me."

Chapter Seventeen

When Jalesia arrived at Derrick's house, there were red rose petals on the front porch. There was a huge note on the door, "Come in and follow the rose petals. I have something in store for you." The petals led to the dinning room table and on the table were a dozen of red roses and another note. "Have I told you lately that I love you? Follow the petals to the guest bedroom." The petals led to the bed, and on the bed was Jalesia's outfit for the evening. Derrick had bought her a black suit, white shirt, and black low-heel pumps. Attached to the outfit was another note, "I love you with all my heart. Pick up your suit and continue to follow the petals to the master suite." Jalesia loved the fact that Derrick is finally telling her that he loves her.

The rose petals led to the bed in the master suite. On the bed was a gold, heart shape lock. There was a key in the middle of the heart shape lock and another note, "Leave my heart on the dresser, and the key is yours. You now have the key to my heart. I hope you don't loose it nor throw it away. Continue to follow the rose petals."

Jalesia had no ideal what Derrick was up to, but she was enjoying every moment. The rose petals led outside on the patio. On the table was a small black velvet box and another note, "Do you love me? If you love me, pick up this box, come inside of the garage, and get into the Bentley. You can cash the box in for Derrick Dubois delicious kiss or you can have what's inside the box."

Jalesia knew Derrick well enough that if she showed him how important he was, he would do anything for her. Even though she wanted to open the box, she did not.

When Jalesia arrived inside the garage, Derrick was sitting in the Bentley with his head tilted back. Jalesia leaned inside the car to give Derrick a kiss and she must have startled him because he jumped. Jalesia's voice was filled with excitement,

"Hello sweetheart, I would like to cash in this velvet box."

Derrick stepped out of the car to give Jalesia a hug,

"You mean to tell me that you would rather have a kiss from me, than what is in the box?"

"Yes sir. That box cannot hold the importance of a Derrick Dubois kiss right now."

Derrick pulled Jalesia into his arms and kissed her enough to make up for the times they have spent apart from one another. He took the box and placed it in the glove compartment,

"Good choice, because there is nothing in the velvet box. Sweetheart, I love you."

Jalesia wiped her lip-gloss from Derrick's lips,

"Derrick, I love you too."

Derrick was so excited to see Jalesia that he could not keep his hands and mouth off of her. Derrick asked,

"Are you ready to go?"

"Yes I am ready for what ever you have in mind. I know you have my best interest in mind."

Derrick looked deep into Jalesia's eyes and said,

"I really do love you."

When Derrick and Jalesia arrived at Orlando's Walt Disney World Resort, he already had their hotel and dinner reservations. Jalesia recommended to Derrick to stay at the hotel instead of going to the night parade. She wanted to spend some quiet quality time with Derrick. But that was not Derrick's plan. He recommended they continue with the plans he had made.

After getting dressed, they went to the Magic Kingdom for the light show and night parade. Derrick knew exactly where he needed to be standing for the light show. While watching the light show, suddenly the band stopped playing and the lights went dim. The announcer came on the PA system and announced,

"Attention all Walt Disney World Guest, we are glad so many of you have come out to share this very special event. We need everyone to participate. Please reach inside of your jacket pocket to see if you have anything inside. When Jalesia reached inside of her pocket, there was a diamond ring. Jalesia started crying. Suddenly the cannons sounded and across the building in bright neon lights read, "Jalesia Anna Brantz, will you marry me, Derrick Curtis Dubois?" Before Jalesia could respond, Mickey Mouse came up holding a microphone and the bright spotlight was on Jalesia. Mickey said,

"If you look straight ahead, you will see yourself on the giant screen. Everyone including Derrick Dubois will know your answer."

The tears were falling from Jalesia's eyes and she was trembling with excitement,

"Yes Derrick, I will marry you."

The cannons sounded and the fire works lit up the sky. The crowd erupted with cheers.

This had to be one of the best days of Jalesia's life. After different ones congratulated them, Derrick finally made it official. Derrick balanced himself on one knee and proposed. Looking up at Jalesia with the most serious look on his face,

"Jalesia, will you marry me?"

Jalesia looked down at Derrick,

"I have not changed my mind, my answer is still yes. Yes, I will marry you."

Derrick stood up and hugged Jalesia tightly, and they engaged in a deeply romantic kiss.

The two and a half carat, heart shape, diamond ring was beautiful. While at dinner, different people would approach Derrick and Jalesia to congratulate them on their engagement. Jalesia was admiring her ring as the lights shinning on the diamond caused the ring to sparkle.

As soon as they returned to their room, Jalesia could not wait to call Rosa.

"Mother, it is official. Derrick and I are engaged! He continues to tell me that he loves me. Derrick told me that you helped him picked out the ring and my outfit. Mother thanks for all that you do."

"Oh Lea, I want what is best for you. I am not going to hold you up, get back to your soon to be husband, and we can have this conversation later."

After hanging up the phone, Jalesia joined Derrick on the sofa. The mood was perfect for cuddling. When Jalesia looked at Derrick, she did not understand the puzzled look on his face.

Jalesia asked,

"Are you okay? You seem to be deep in thoughts."

"I'm okay, but you are correct. I am deep in thoughts. We need to talk."

Jalesia put her arms around Derrick and laid back in his arms,

"Tell me what is on your mind my soon to be husband."

Derrick began to address his concerns as he brushed Jalesia's hair with his hand.

"First of all, I don't want to rush our engagement. I want you to finish college and accomplish all the things you desire. I will not pressure you, and I know you will not pressure me. I have taken a deeper stand with the Lord. I remember you told me that you feel the Lord is calling you deeper in the ministry. I have prayed about some things, and the Lord showed me that you are a chosen vessel in this ministry. At first I could not get behind a woman in ministry because of my religious up bringing. But now I am a believer in the ministry God has called you into. I want you to know, I support you one hundred percent. When we have prayer together, and you're praying, I can feel the anointing of God all over you."

Jalesia squeezed Derrick and held him tightly,

"I have to be one of the most blessed women in the world to have a man like you. Thank you sweetheart for understanding."

Chapter Eighteen

*J*alesia had decided not to take any of the offers for a career job. She had talked with Derrick and Pastor Hamilton about going full time in the ministry. Pastor Hamilton explained to Jalesia that the church does not recognize female Pastors, but he had the perfect job for her. He recommended the Department of Evangelism. Derrick did not agree with Pastor Hamilton, because he felt if he could have a change of heart about females preaching, then anyone should. He felt women are just as anointed and used of the Lord as men.

College days are now over. The only thing left to do is go back for the graduation ceremonies. Jalesia had completed her last test and since she knew Derrick was going to be in New York for the weekend, she decided to pay him a surprise visit.

Jalesia's flight was scheduled to leave Miami going to New York, with an arrival time of 8:00 p.m. in New York. When Jalesia arrived in New York, all the limousines were full. She decided to take a cab to Derrick's apartment complex. When Jalesia saw the cab driver get on the interstate, she became a little concern. "Derrick never had to board the free way to get to his apartments."

Jalesia tried to stop the cab driver,

"Excuse me Sir, you may have taken the wrong turn because this is not the way to Dubois Estate Community."

The angry cab driver answered back with an Arabic accent,

"I know where you asked me to take you, but I need to go somewhere else first."

Jalesia was beginning to be a little upset,

"Sir, would you please take me back to the airport? I will have someone to pick me up from there."

The cab driver kept going farther away. When he exited off the freeway and turned into a low housing development, Jalesia knew this was not her destination. Most of the units in the community were boarded up. The streets were very dark.

The cab driver stepped out of the car with a knife in his hand and demanded Jalesia to get out of the cab and hand him all of her jewelry. When Jalesia was forced to take off her engagement ring, she began to cry. After the cab driver robbed Jalesia, he hurried back into his car and sped away.

Jalesia was crying as she walked down the street not knowing where she was headed. She was in the middle of nowhere. It was dark, cold, and very spooky. Jalesia had walked until she finally came to an apartment where the lights were on. She walked on the porch and knocked on the door. An elderly lady answered the door,

"Come on in baby, how can I help you?"

Before Jalesia could respond someone came up behind her and pushed her to the floor. The door slammed behind her.

The cold, harsh, angry voice screamed at Jalesia as she starred back into the barrel of the gun.

"I want you to shut up and not say a word and you could probably make it out of here alive."

The tears started rolling down Jalesia's face. She was trembling, trying to reason with the man,

"Sir, I have nothing. I was just robbed, but if you let me go, I will get you anything you want."

The man started talking through clenched teeth,

"I told you to shut up, don't say another word, and both of you take off all you clothes."

The old lady tried to grab the gun. The angry man hit her with the handle of the gun. She was knocked unconscious and her forehead was split. The man grew angrier as he yelled at Jalesia,

"I told you to take off all your clothes. DO IT NOW!"

Jalesia was not moving fast enough. The man grabbed the neck of the dress, and ripped it open. Jalesia was exposed with just her bra and panties. Without warning, he grabbed her by the hair and threw her to the floor. When he pounced on her, his knee hit Jalesia in the stomach. At this point, Jalesia knew this monster was too much for her to handle, especially since he had a gun.

Jalesia tried to fight back, kicking, waving, screaming and scratching. When the man pulled back on the trigger, he forced the gun in Jalesia's mouth. Jalesia lifted her hands in complete surrender.

The man with the hard, rough voice spoke with a lot of anger,

"If I tell you one more time about screaming, I promise, I will kill you."

The man then punched Jalesia a few times splitting her lip. With his fist he then punched her in the stomach. The pain was so excruciating Jalesia could not move. The blood started to trickle from the corners of Jalesia's mouth.

The man then straddled Jalesia as he unzipped his pants and ripped off Jalesia's bra and panties. Jalesia remained motionless as the man starred into her eyes and she starred back into his disgusting hate filled eyes. She could feel the warm tears rolling backwards, down her cheeks, past her ears and neck.

Jalesia began to shake in fear. She squeezed her eyes tightly as the nasty beast pulled her legs apart. She began to cry out loud,

"Oh God! Please God, don't allow this to happen to me. Please God, I need your help."

She let out a loud cry once the man entered into her. The man moaned and groaned as he moved up and down, hard and harder, on top of her. Jalesia tried squirming under the pressure of his weight. She lies there gasping for air, trying to catch her breath.

The pain from the penetration was so severe. She thought she was dying. Jalesia began to ask the Lord,

"Lord, why would you allow this to happen to me? Oh God this really hurts, Please Lord help me. God make him stop."

As the cruel and foul man continued to pounce, thrust in and out, and yet harder and harder, Jalesia began to quote the 71st Psalm,

"In Thee O Lord, do I put my trust; let me never be put to confusion. Deliver me in thy righteousness, and cause me to escape;

incline Thine ear unto me; and save me. Be Thou my strong habitation, where unto I may continually resort; Thou have given Commandment to save me, for thou art my rock and fortress. Deliver me O my God out of the hand of the wicked, out of the hand of the unrighteous and cruel man."

When the disgusting, wicked animal released his seed, he stood up and looked at Jalesia, spit in her face and said,

"I should have killed you, but you ain't worth it."

Before the man walked out the door, he walked over to the old lady and urinated on her.

Jalesia was in too much pain to move. She was crying uncontrollably,

"Why Lord, this is not how it was suppose to be. All the men I have turned away and you allowed this to happen to me. Why did it have to happen this way? Why Lord, Why?"

Jalesia was hurting so badly that she could not get up. She struggled to crawl to the phone and dialed 911. She reported that she had been raped and an elderly woman had been assaulted. Jalesia explained to the operator that she did not know where she was located. The operator asked her to stay on the line until the paramedics arrived.

When the paramedics finally arrived, Jalesia was too weak to do anything. She was naked, with the exception of a ripped dress. When the paramedic rushed in with the gurney, they wrapped a sheet around Jalesia's naked body, and lifted her off the floor. There was a small puddle of blood on the floor where Jalesia's body was.

One of the medics left Jalesia and went to assist the elderly lady. Her face was covered with blood and she was now gaining conscious. The medic asked,

"What happened here? I need names and details of what took place."

Jalesia was too weak to talk, but the old lady answered with her voice just above a whisper,

"Some man broke into my apartment, he said to rape and kill me. This lady just so happen to be walking by and she must have heard the man yelling and screaming, so she came up to see about me. The young lady was raped and beaten pretty bad. I can say she saved my life."

By this time the detectives arrived on the scene and began to ask questions. The medic interrupted,

"What ever you need to ask her will have to wait until we get her to the hospital. She has lost a lot of blood and we need to stabilize her and get her to the hospital immediately."

The medic secured Jalesia into the ambulance and rushed to the hospital with the sirens blaring, and speeding through the dark streets.

Chapter Nineteen

*T*he doctor came to Jalesia's bed side and laid her hand on Jalesia's shoulder,

"I'm Dr. Morris and I will be the one to take care of you."

Dr. Morris was a medium brown skin tone woman with a smooth complexion. She was wearing a long white jacket over a yellow dress.

The nurse came in the room and put the blood pressure cup on Jalesia's arm.

The doctor continued as she looked down at Jalesia with a concern look on her face.

"I am going to ask you some questions, but the first thing I want to do is get you into the X-ray room so we can run some test to see what is causing the vaginal bleeding."

After the X-rays, the MRI, and the CT-scan, Dr. Morris came into the room holding Jalesia's charts,

"Ma-am, we don't have any information on you, but we wanted to get the test done in the event that we need to perform surgery. The results came back negative. There were no signs of any head trauma, even though you suffered a few blows to the head causing a minor concussion. Due to your ruptured cervical, you do have some minor bleeding. We are going to keep you for observation, because you continue to black out. We need to monitor your stomach area for any internal injuries. I'm going to send someone in here to get your name, and insurance information, and I will come back to explain what we are going to be doing."

Before Dr. Morris walked out, Jalesia spoke to her just barley above a whisper,

"Dr. Morris?"

Dr. Morris gently lifted Jalesia's hand between her hands.

"My name is Jalesia Anna Brantz and this all happened so fast. I live in Florida and I was flying out to New York to surprise my fiancé. The cab driver robbed me and left me in the heart of the low income housing projects."

Dr. Morris slightly squeezed Jalesia's hand and said,

"Miss Brantz, I specialize in taking care of women who has been beaten or raped. Now once we get your information, I will come back in here to ask you some questions, and do a physical for rape survivors. I want you to understand, once I'm done you will be interviewed by detectives, and that is not always pleasant, because you may feel interrogated. Listen, I will be back and I will go over everything with you. I promise, you will have my undivided attention."

As Dr. Morris turned to walk away, Jalesia grabbed her by the hand and pulled her back by her side. The tears were rolling down Jalesia's cheeks as she spoke,

"Dr. Morris, tell me the truth, how does my face look?"

Dr. Morris hesitated, and then responded with a sound of uncertainty,

"Your face is fine. Of course you have a few scratches, and a minor split in your bottom lip. Your cheekbones are swollen and around your eyes are black and blue, but you will heal just fine. The bruises are superficial, and they will heal in a few days. I promise you, I will return and we will discuss every minor detail. Do you want me to notify your fiancé, your mother, any friends or family members?"

Jalesia responded as she began to cry again,

"No, at this point I don't want anyone to know what I have gone through, I am too embarrassed and hurt right now."

When Dr. Morris came back into the room, Jalesia was able to muster up a smile through her pain. Dr. Morris pulled a stool beside Jalesia's bed, and she placed Jalesia's hand between her hands and said,

"I want you to be as comfortable as possible. Some of the questions are going to hurt, but I need you to be as thorough as possible. I am here for you as your doctor and your sister in Christ."

Jalesia smiled again,

"Wow! How did you know?"

Dr. Morris smiled at Jalesia,

"I know because only God can give the peace that you have right now. Understand, I deal with this type of situation on a daily basis, and I know my sisters. Would you like to begin telling me what happened? I am sure you will cover every question I need to ask."

When Jalesia told the story in its entirety, Dr. Morris explained the remaining procedure,

"You are very special to me, and I will not be leaving your side. I will be here from start to finish. Every test that is performed, I will be there. I understand you. You are in the exact same situation I was in. We will complete a physical, after which we will need to take photos with your consent. Forensic evidence will detail menstrual history, pelvic exam, marks, bruises, sperm cells, and fingernail scraping. This will give us the information that we will need, such as; blood, fluids, semen, and pubic hairs. We will check for any sexually transmitted disease, and we will need to draw blood for an aids test."

Jalesia could feel the warm tears rolling down her cheeks as she swallowed hard the lump that was in her throat.

Dr. Morris continued,

"We have an excellent rape counseling program that is conducted by me."

Jalesia was shaking her head,

"No, I will not be needing counseling. I am going to lean extra heavy on the Lord, and I know he will bring me through this."

Jalesia blacked out, and Dr. Morris monitored her stats while she was out. When Jalesia came to, Dr. Morris asked her a few questions,

"Do you know where you are? Do you know what happened to you?"

Jalesia responded as she held her hand up to her head,

"I know I am in a hospital in New York. I have been raped and beaten, and right now I am in so much pain I don't know what to do. I would probably be able to suffer through some of the soreness if I could get something for my headache."

Dr. Morris brushed Jalesia hair back from her face,

"I have been monitoring you, and you are under a lot of pressure. Before you blacked out I was speaking to you about counseling. I will be willing to do some one on one counseling with you, free of charge. I understand your walk with the Lord, and that is the reason He has given people to be helpers one with another. The trauma that you have experienced is not easy. You may encounter flashbacks, feelings of depression, nightmares, or any feeling out of the ordinary. God is able to give you the strength that you need, and He has also placed His instruments in places to assist. We will discuss that later, because I know I am not going to have any problems out of you. I am going to be your doctor, your friend, and your sister in Christ, so I am not concerned about you shaking your head no about counseling. We have no way of providing a pregnancy test, but we can give you a pill that is provided to rape survivors that will abort any pregnancy."

Jalesia started crying again,

"No, I will not take any pills. I just believe God will keep me."

Dr. Morris squeezed Jalesia's hand,

"I understand, but if you feel different, we can provide that for you."

After all the test were done, the scraping, taking blood, interrogation, Jalesia was completely worn out, and day break had started coming through the window. Jalesia was too exhausted to keep her eyes opened, and fell into a deep sleep.

"Please God, when I awake, let all of this be a bad dream."

Chapter Twenty

*D*r. Morris came into Jalesia's room and opened the curtains. The bright light caused Jalesia to squint her eyes as she spoke with surprise,

"Good-afternoon Dr. Morris. I guess I did not have a bad dream after all."

Dr. Morris responded,

"No, unfortunately it was not a bad dream. I will need you to try walking around today. I realize you're going to move slowly, and you will be extremely sore, but you must improve in order to go home."

"Dr. Morris, will I be going home today?"

Dr. Morris reached for Jalesia charts at the foot of her bed,

"You have a very bad bruised stomach, and the vagina will take some time to heal. I had to add some sutures, because with this being your first time, and it was a very rough experience, you had a minor tear. You also have inflammation and irritation of the cervix and to the entrance of the vagina."

Jalesia looked at Dr. Morris with her eyebrows raised,

"It is unbelievable how you can know so much about a person, because I did not tell you that I was a virgin."

Dr. Morris smiled,

"Some things are spiritual, like knowing you are my sister in Christ, and some things are from being a doctor. Knowing you were a virgin is not spiritual, but doctor wit."

Jalesia tried getting up, and Dr. Morris assisted her,

"I am going to do the best I can to get mobilized, because I really want to go home."

Dr. Morris placed her hand on top of Jalesia's hand,

"I am going to leave for a couple of hours, but I will come back to see how you are doing. Today, and tomorrow are my off days, but when I told you I would be with you from start to finish, I meant exactly what I said."

Jalesia stood up, and began walking around. When Jalesia passed a mirror and saw herself, she began crying and went back to her room.

When Dr. Morris returned she had in her hands a denim dress, a leather jacket, under garments, a pair of flat shoes, and a pair of sunglasses,

"Since I knew I was releasing you today, I picked up a few items that you would need. I have already made your flight arrangements, and I will be taking you to the airport. I told you, you are my sister in Christ."

After Jalesia got dressed to go home, she called her mother so that she would meet her at the airport in Tampa at 5:45. When Rosa answered the phone, her voice sounded like she had been crying,

"Lea, where are you? We have been worried all night about you. Derrick has checked every airline, bus station, and train station looking for you. Derrick is in Tampa, because he had a feeling you would be coming home early. He wanted to be here when you got home. He told me he has not gotten any sleep, and neither have I. Your roommate, Tracy, told us that you left Miami going to New York so that you could surprise Derrick. Derrick has been crying, saying that it is his fault that you are missing. Your father took off from work, because he had been out all night looking for you.

Your brothers, Otis Junior and Edward are out looking for you. We all have not been able to rest. I had a peace to come over me this morning. I told everyone that you were all right and we will be hearing from you today. Baby, I know for a fact that the Lord gave me that peace. I know that what ever you had to go through this morning around six o'clock, you had peace of mind, because that is when the Lord gave me peace. Other than what you had to go through, is everything all right?"

Jalesia answered with a short, snappy response,

"No Mother, everything is not all right, this has been the worst day of my life, and I do not want to talk about it. I have had enough of interrogations for one day, and all I want to do is get home and lock up in my room. I do not want to talk to anyone right now. Please don't tell Derrick you have heard from me, because I do not want to see him right now. I am in a lot of pain. I was robbed and beaten, and that's all I want to say right now. I am leaving the hospital now heading home. Please, pick me up from the airport alone. I do not want anyone to see me like this."

Rosa answered,

"I will be there at 5:45."

Dr. Morris took Jalesia to the airport, and in route to the airport, Dr. Morris explained,

"Jalesia, I am going to give you my home phone number, my work number, my cell phone number, and my pager, so you will be able to contact me at any time if you need me. I was married when I was raped, and it took me about two months before Michael and I were intimate again, and I was not able to enjoy him until the third month. Counseling is good for both of you. Your fiancé will need to know how to handle you once he makes love to you. You may experience all types of mood swings, and he will need to know that you are affected mentally and emotionally. There were days I would cry just thinking about what happened to me."

Jalesia laid her head on Dr. Morris's shoulder,

"Dr. Morris, I know exactly what you are saying, because I had a rough time sleeping this morning just thinking about what I have gone through."

"Jalesia, call me Zephanie and not Dr. Morris. You don't have to call me for counseling, but you can call me as your friend, and we can talk."

Chapter Twenty-one

$\mathcal{T}$he flight home was exhausting. Jalesia was in so much pain. The seat belt was painful on her stomach, the stitches were painful to sit on, her head was pounding, and her mouth was sore.

When Jalesia arrived at Tampa International Airport, Rosa was already there. As soon as Jalesia saw Rosa, she started crying. Rosa did not help the situation, because she started crying also. Rosa ran over to Jalesia and wrapped her arms around her,

"What in God's green earth has happened to you?"

Jalesia pulled away from Rosa,

"Mother, please don't hug me so tight, I am in so much pain."

"You have had me so worried about you."

Rosa lifted Jalesia sunglasses as she stared into her swollen eyes,

"Baby, tell me what happened. Who did this to you? I hope he burns in hell for doing this to you."

"Mother, please do not make a scene. Just get me home, and I'll explain things to you later. I am sore, I am hurting, I am tired, and I am totally confused. I just want to get home, so I can get some rest."

Rosa took Jalesia by the hand,

"Come on baby, let's get your luggage so I can get you home."

"Mother, I do not have any luggage. I was robbed and everything was taken from me."

Jalesia started crying all over again.

When Jalesia got home she got her silk nightgown and headed for the bathtub to take a long hot soak. She still felt unclean. When Jalesia lie back in the tub, and closed her eyes, the only thing she could think about was the monster that had beaten and raped her. She also thought about how he had taken the one thing from her that she treasured the most, which was her virginity.

How would she be able to tell anyone what happened to her. As Jalesia thought long and hard about the situation, she felt so embarrassed to even think about it, let alone to tell someone about it.

Dr. Morris, Zephanie, was right, the flashbacks kept coming back and Jalesia was crying and praying to God,

"Oh God, I need your help right now. This is so much for me to endure. Please Lord, come into my mind, and help to rid these thoughts, touch my body and heal all my pains. I need you Lord like never before. I don't understand why I had to go through this, but you know, and all I'm asking is for you to help me to go through."

There was a knock on the bathroom door. Jalesia had been in the tub for a long time. Her fingers and toes were white and wrinkled.

"Who is it?"

Rosa shouted back through the door.

"Lea, baby, it's me, you have been in the tub for a long time, and I just wanted to know if you are okay? Derrick called and I did not know what to tell him. He asked me to tell you to call him once you're done. When you come out, I want to tuck you in the bed, so you can get some rest. Your father told me to tell you he wants to see you for a brief moment once you are done."

"Mother, I will be out in a few minutes."

After taking her bath Jalesia went into her bedroom and got in her bed. There was a big knuckle knock at her door. Jalesia knew it was not her mother. She got under the covers,

"Come on in, the door is unlocked."

Otis walked in with a frown on his face,

"Tell me who did it, and I will make it my business to get to New York, and somebody is dead." Otis sat on the bed next to Jalesia, with tears in his eyes. "Lea, I need to know. Don't withhold this information from me. Who did this to you?"

Jalesia knew her father was serious. If he could get his hands on the man that was responsible for her pain, he would be a dead man. Jalesia knew she did not want her father to get into any trouble trying to find the person who hurt her, even though she would have loved to see him near dead right now herself. Jalesia reached for her father's hand,

"Father, I don't know who did it, after the man beat me, he ran away. The man had a gun and I am grateful he did not shoot me. The detectives are investigating this incident, and as soon as they get more information they will call me. The detectives explained, once they apprehend the suspect they will need me to go to New York to identify him. Don't worry Father, everything will be alright."

Rosa walked into the room,

"Otis, let her get her rest, we can talk about all of this tomorrow."

Otis stood up and walked out of the room. Rosa stayed back to tuck Jalesia in. Jalesia asked,

"Mother, do I look that bad?"

"Baby, it does look bad. Your entire face is swollen, and around your eyes are black and blue, but I know you will recover in a couple of days. Get your rest, I will fix you breakfast in the morning and we can talk then."

Rosa and Otis were talking when suddenly there was a knock on the front door. Otis answered the door, and it was Derrick,

"Good evening Mr. And Mrs. Brantz, how is Jalesia doing? Can I see her?"

Otis answered,

"Derrick, I realize she will soon be your wife, but she asked that no one see her tonight, and I know you will respect her request."

"Yes sir, I will respect her request, but is she alright?"

Otis put his hand on Derrick's shoulder,

"Son, let me put it like this, I have seen much better days for my baby, and if I could get my hands on the man that did this, he would be a dead man."

Otis turned towards his bedroom,

"I will leave this discussion for you and Kid to talk about." Otis called Rosa Kid. "I need to go to bed so I can get up and go to work in the morning."

After Otis left the room, Rosa looked up at Derrick,

"Derrick, she does not want anyone to see her, and if she was not so tired I would let you. I know you care about her, and you have her best interest in mind, but she asked us to please let her sleep."

Derrick put his hands in his pockets as he paced the floor,

"Mother, I love Jalesia, and I am very concern about her. I am so sorry she wanted to come out to New York to surprise me. This hurts me more than you will ever know, and the fact that I was unable to protect her, hurts even worst." The tears fell from Derrick's eyes. "Mother, let me go in just for a minute, to hug and comfort her, and to let her know that I love her, and I am here for her."

Rosa answered,

"Derrick, I understand your love for her, and I will tell her how concern you were for her, but she asked me to let her rest, and she would talk with us in the morning. I love my baby, and she even asked me if I would leave her room."

Derrick was pacing the floor with his hands intertwined behind his head,

"Mother, how bad is it? Did she give you any information? What could you see?"

Rosa tilted her head back and started crying. Derrick sat next to her and put his arm around her, and Rosa answered,

"It's not that bad, but it is bad. I have never seen my baby like this before. Her face is swollen, her eyes are black and blue, she has some scratches on her face, her lip is split, and she is walking extremely slowly. She did tell me how much pain she was in. I think she said that she was punched and kicked in her stomach." Rosa started crying harder. She spoke through her sobbing, "How could anyone be so brutal to her? I know my baby did nothing to deserve this."

Derrick held Rosa in his arms as he rocked back and forth,

"It's going to be alright. We don't always understand why things happen when it happens, but I believe God will be glorified in this situation. Jalesia is strong, and she will get through this and we will be there for her, and with her."

Rosa and Derrick continued to talk, and Derrick finally stood up to leave,

"I am going to leave and go home, because as soon as I can

come over I will be here with the quickness. Let my sweetheart know that I love her, and I wanted nothing more than to tell her myself, but you and Pops would not let me."

Rosa stood up to escort Derrick out the door and said,

"You know what Derrick, I would be less than a mother to you not to let you see Lea tonight. I am going to allow you to see her, but just be brief, and try not to wake her."

Derrick walked into the room. Jalesia was asleep. He knelt down next to her bed and kissed her on the forehead and said,

"Jalesia, I love you, and I am here for you."

Jalesia did not open her eyes, but she pulled one of her hands from under the covers and extended it to Derrick. Derrick kissed Jalesia's hand, then kissed her on the forehead again, and stood up to walk out the door. Jalesia responded in a mere whisper,

"Derrick, I love you too."

Rosa walked Derrick to the door. He turned and hugged her.

Rosa softly replied,

"Derrick thanks for everything. You are going to make a mighty fine son. I am going to need your help, because when Lea's brothers hear about this, they are going to declare war, but we must do what is right. Pray and ask God for strength to go through this and to bring this person to justice, and let God work things out in His way and in His time."

Chapter Twenty-two

$\mathcal{R}$osa was already up and had cooked breakfast. She went into Jalesia's room and opened the curtains,

"Good-morning baby, how are you feeling today? If you get up and get dressed, you will feel better."

Jalesia rolled over slowly and pulled the covers over her head. She responded to the question with a muffled sound through the covers,

"I was doing a lot better until you opened the curtains."

Rosa walked over to Jalesia's bed and gently placed her hand on her shoulder,

"The sun is good for you. It gives you back your strength and makes your day brighter. Come on and get up. I have prepared you a heartfelt, love filled breakfast. Your fiancé called this morning and he is on his way over."

Jalesia began to whine,

"Mother, I don't want Derrick to see me like this. I had no intentions on putting on clothes today. I wanted to just lay around and rest."

Rosa sat on the bed next to Jalesia and put her arms around her,

"Baby, you have yourself a fine young Christian man, and that boy loves you. Not for the way you look, but you have gotten into his heart, and that is a different kind of love. I had a chance to see the real Derrick last night. The man really does love you, and he was hurting for you last night. He begged me to let him go into your room, just so he could tell you that he loves you and he is here for you."

Rosa reached over to help Jalesia sit up on the side of her bed and she continued,

"Derrick told me that he wish he could carry those pains for you, and how he has never loved any one as much has he loves you. Yes, I let him go into the room to see you last night. I told him he was more than welcome to come over this morning to talk with you. I want him to get the story on what happened to you the same time you tell me."

Jalesia buried her face in her hand and began to cry,

"Mother, after I tell you and Derrick about what happened, please do not ask any questions. I do not want to go through another day of interrogation."

After Jalesia got up and freshened up, she put on a big dress to lounge around in. Jalesia and Rosa ate breakfast and were sitting in the living room talking when Derrick came up.

When Derrick walked in he greeted Rosa. He walked over to the sofa and softly kissed Jalesia on the forehead then sat next to her,

"Good-morning sweetheart. I love you."

Jalesia responded,

"Good-morning Derrick, I love you too."

Jalesia told Rosa and Derrick everything except for being raped. She could not tell them that she had been raped, because she was too embarrassed. Jalesia was crying uncontrollably because she had to relive that whole scene in her head again. Derrick spoke softly with his deep soothing voice as he rocked Jalesia in his arms,

"Sssshhh!!! It's going to be all right. As I said before I am here for you. I love you. You don't ever have to worry about how you look with me, because I know my sweetheart is cute. That little swelling and those few scratches will heal, and you will be back to normal in no time. I did not fall in love with your beauty. I fell in love with the woman within. I know you were telling us that Dr. Morris said she would like to follow up on your conditions, to make sure you did not sustain any internal injuries. I love you for you. So don't ever worry about being able to produce children that should be the least of your worries. God has all the things we can't handle under control. We don't worry, we place it in God's hands."

Something kept telling Jalesia to tell Derrick and Rosa everything, but she could not do it. She knew she needed to call Zephanie because she could not get that nasty feeling off of her. Jalesia could still see the rapist face, his evil eyes, and the flashbacks were still there.

Rosa stood up to walk out of the room,

"I am going to leave you two alone to talk because I have to do laundry today."

Derrick laid one hand on Jalesia's stomach,

"What did the doctor say about internal injuries? Do you have more test that needs to be done?"

"I don't have any test that needs to be done right now. Zephanie will review the test that has already been done and will contact me to go over the results. Derrick, if I can't have any children, I can understand you not wanting to be with me."

Derrick looked at Jalesia with his mouth pushed out and his forehead wrinkled,

"You have made me angry, and slapped me in my face. Why in the world would you say something like that? Do you think I love you and want to marry you because you look like you can have babies? What if I could not produce any babies, would you not want me?"

Jalesia put her hand on Derrick's cheek and dropped her head,

"I'm sorry honey, I did not mean it like that. I know how you have told me that you wanted to have children, and I was just thinking about you."

Derrick placed Jalesia hand in his hand,

"I love you. If we have children, that's fine and if we don't have children, it's still fine. No one can perform that miracle but God. I am concern about you and your health. "

Derrick held out his hand for Jalesia,

"Honey, come go home with me, and let me take care of you. I want to protect you and nurse you back to health."

Jalesia took a deep breath,

"Derrick, I know you love me, but I am too tired. You have lost your mind if you think mother is going to let me leave here. She will not have it."

Rosa was walking back into the room and asked,

"Sounds like you two were talking about me. What is it that I won't have?"

Jalesia put her hand over her ears because she knew Derrick was about to get it. He then answered,

"Mother, I asked Jalesia to go home with me so I can take care of her and nurse her back to health."

Jalesia was sitting quietly shaking her head, because she knew Derrick was about to get it. However, Rosa had a smile on her face and said,

"Son, sweetie pie, I am going to let you have this nice and easy, because you don't know me like that. I am most capable of nursing my child back to health, and that is what I plan to do. You are not married, and do understand if you were, this is my baby, and I love her more than you will ever know. I know the word of God, how a person is to leave mother and father and cleave to his wife or her husband, and they are to be as one. I can go along with that because that is the word of God, but nowhere do you see that the mother has to change her way of loving her children. God has left that part up to the mothers to decide how to handle herself. Being a mother, you should know how to conduct yourself at all times, and in all situations."

Derrick held up his hands in surrender as his lips spread into a wide grin,

"Okay, Okay. It was just a thought. I will just have to make your life miserable by coming over here all the time."

Rosa was standing with her hands on her hip,

"Now my son is back to normal, at one point I was concerned for you, thinking you were going to march out the door with my baby."

Changing the conversation, Jalesia interrupted,

"Derrick, would you pass me the phone and look on my bed and bring me that hospital portfolio. I need to call Detective Washington and Zephanie."

Jalesia called Detective Washington first,

"Detective Washington, my name is Jalesia Brantz from Tampa,

Florida. You are working on a case for me."

The deep husky voice responded back through the receiver,

Oh yea! I know who you are, and I was hoping you would call me. We believe we know who the suspect is. We just haven't been able to apprehend him yet. The saliva and the semen is what helped us with the DNA testing. This man has been on the run for some time now, and we believe we know his where about. The medics were able to bottle the saliva from your face, which was a perfect lead for us.

Jalesia put her hand up to her face,

"Oh yea, I had forgotten all about that nasty man spitting in my face. But now I remember. He did that just before he walked out of the door. He told me that he hated me, and then he spit in my face."

Detective Washington commented,

"One more thing before I let you go. Everyone is calling you a hero, especially the elderly lady that you rescued. She wants to do something special for you. This man has raped and beaten several elderly women. I will contact you once we have this guy in custody. We will need you to come back to New York to identify him."

Jalesia was able to smile,

"Detective Washington, thanks, that is almost the best news I have heard all day. Keep me posted and as soon as you hear something, let me know, and I will be there."

"You are welcome. Good bye"

"Bye-Bye."

Derrick, Rosa, and Jalesia had talked all afternoon about the wedding plans. As the day got later, Jalesia began to feel depressed. She was having flashbacks and could not get the rapist face out of her mind.

As Jalesia started to get up, but still in too much pain to get up alone, Derrick rushed over and took her by one arm to help her up. Jalesia was grimacing in pain,

"I need to lay down. I am in so much pain. I am going to get into my bed, and get some rest."

Derrick helped Jalesia get into the bed and he tucked her in. Derrick brushed Jalesia's hair from her face. He gently kissed her on the forehead and said,

"Jalesia, I am going to take care of some business. Do you need me to bring you any thing?"

Jalesia answered,

"No, I will be fine, just be careful out there. Are you coming back by later on?"

"No, I am not coming back by. I will come over in the morning, but I will call you later tonight. Do you think you will be up to talking?"

"No, I will not be up to talking tonight, so go on home, and get your rest and I will see you on tomorrow."

Derrick walked out of Jalesia's room and Rosa walked him to the door. Derrick hugged Rosa and said,

Mother, thanks for everything that you do. I really appreciate you. You are going to be a wonderful mother-in-law. I am so glad we get along like we do now, because this is how we will get along when Jalesia and I get married. I really do love her, and I thank you for always being there to listen to me, as well as listening to her. You don't take the side of your children, but you're fair, and that is what's important. I am not going to call tonight. I will let Jalesia get her rest, but I will be over here in the morning."

Rosa hugged Derrick again and said,

"Good night son, I will see you in the morning."

Chapter Twenty-three

The next few days were spent resting and healing. Jalesia was walking around feeling better, but she was still sore. She was sitting on the bed when the telephone rang. Jalesia answered the phone,

"Hello?"

"This is Dr. Morris, may I speak with Jalesia Brantz?"

"This is she."

"Jalesia, this is Zephanie. How have you been? I have been worried about you, and you fell on my heart today, so I had to call you."

Jalesia hesitated,

"I have been okay, some days are better than others."

Zephanie's voice was full of excitement,

"I put in a transfer to Florida, and I will be moving there in the next month."

Jalesia was excited and curious,

"Wow, what would make you do that?"

"You."

"Me? How did I make you do that?"

Zephanie was sitting at her desk in her office. She swirled around in her chair and said,

"You were my angel. Michael and I had always talked about moving to Florida, because that's where he is originally from. I never would make the move to Florida, because I always felt I did not know anyone there, but now I know you."

"Zephanie, that is really special. I thought you were only kidding when you asked me about being your friend, but now I see you were for real."

Zephanie was smiling from ear to ear and said,

"Michael and I had been holding off from buying a house in New York, and as soon as I told him I wanted to move to Florida, he started working on getting a house in Florida. I don't want to talk about Michael and our adventure. I want to talk about you. You were on my mind, and I want to know about you."

Jalesia could not wait for Zephanie to allow her the opportunity to speak,

"Zephanie, the last couple of days has been rough, sleeping at night is miserable. I toss and turn all night long. I am constantly praying asking God to let me have a peaceful night of sleep."

Zephanie sat up so she could listen to Jalesia attentively,

"Do you live alone, or are you living with ummm... Zephanie snapped her finger, "Derrick?"

Jalesia had a surprised tone,

"No, I don't live with Derrick. I have spent the night with him before, but Rosa does not play that."

Zephanie became concerned and said,

"Well, what you need to do is have your mother sleep with you. I need to know if you are talking or fighting in your sleep. After you have gone through a trauma like this, every detail is important."

Jalesia buried her face in her hands,

"I have not told anyone yet about being raped. What if I am saying something about being raped in my sleep? I do not want anyone to know. This is an embarrassing situation."

Zephanie stood up from her desk and looked out the window.

"I tell you what, Michael and I will be down there next Friday, and I will sleep in the room with you so I can monitor what you are doing in your sleep. Do you think you will be all right until then?"

Zephanie and Jalesia continued their conversation, for nearly an hour, before Zephanie remembered she has patients waiting.

"Jalesia we will continue this conversation next Friday. Take care of yourself, and I will see you then."

"Okay Zephanie, if I need you between now and then, I will call you. Bye-Bye"

"Good bye."

Chapter Twenty-four

*T*he next eleven days were spent continuing resting and healing for Jalesia. Everyday Derrick would come over, and they would talk about their wedding. They had planned a June wedding. Today would be Jalesia's first day out of the house since the rape and the attack incident. Sleeping at night had not gotten any better for Jalesia. She had been waiting for Detective Washington to call. They already knew who the suspect was, and where he was located. They were supposed to make an arrest within the next few days. Jalesia felt once the offender is behind bars, that she could put some closure on all this madness.

It is now Thursday morning. Jalesia had gotten dressed to spend the day with Derrick. Derrick had been extremely nice and patient with Jalesia, but she had been extremely rude to him. Jalesia had also been grumpy and short tempered lately.

Rosa walked into the living room where Jalesia was sitting,

"I think getting out today will help you a great deal, and help me from going off on you. You have been extremely rude lately. Now you see, I am your mother and I will tell you when you are wrong, like it or not. I believe your bad attitude is because of what you have gone through. I guess being locked up in the house for two and a half weeks has caused a change in you. When Derrick asked me did I want to go with you and him to pick out another ring, I definitely did not want to do that. You have been too mean lately, and being apart will do us both some good."

Jalesia did not respond to Rosa's comments, she looked down at her watch and looked back out the window again as her voice snapped,

"Where is he? Derrick should have been here an hour ago. This does not make any sense. I always have to be put on hold lately."

Rosa's voice was low,

"Baby, calm down. I'm sure the man has an excuse. You have been hard on him, and he's doing everything humanly possible to help you get through your ordeal."

Jalesia was holding the cordless phone when it rang. Then she looked at the caller's ID. She pushed out her lips and said,

"This is Derrick calling from his cell phone, and he is not here yet."

Jalesia answered the phone angrily,

"Hello."

Derrick responded in a happy, playful voice,

"How's my baby today? I'm about five minutes away. Sorry I'm late, but I had been with you all week and I needed a haircut and a shave. I stopped by the barber shop to get fixed up for my lady."

Jalesia rolled her eyes and spoke back with a stern voice,

"Derrick, you could have called me. I have been sitting here waiting for you, and do you know how it feels to be shut up in a house this long? I have been waiting, and the least you could have done was to call me."

The phone went dead. Derrick called right back. Jalesia answered,

"Hello."

Derrick was very apologetic,

"Hey, I'm sorry about that, something went wrong with the phone."

Jalesia snapped back,

"Nothing went wrong with the phone. I hung it up. I don't want to hear all of your excuses. I will just see you when you get here. Bye!"

Jalesia disconnected again.

Rosa looked at Jalesia with a frown on her face,

"Lea, I want you to know that you are wrong. Derrick has been doing everything you have asked him to do, and you have been rude. You need to check your attitude. If I were Derrick, I would not put up with your crap."

Rosa got up and walked out of the room.

Derrick was sitting at the red light in his black Lincoln LS. He was waiting for the light to change as he began thinking about Jalesia.

"Hummm! I don't know what has gotten into Jalesia lately, but she is beginning to be a bit ungrateful. I have tried to be nice to her and do anything she has asked of me to help her get through this situation. There is a way to treat the person that is there for you. Maybe we need to discuss the way she has been acting. Perhaps she does not know how I feel. I don't like the way I'm being treated, and to top it all off, she had the nerve to hang up the phone in my face. She has pissed me off. That did it! I will not allow her to get away with that anymore, because she may feel she can get away with anything after this."

When Derrick pulled up in front of the house, Jalesia was looking out the window with a wide grin stretched across her face. She lifted up her hands and said,

"I have got to be a blessed woman, because that is a handsome, fine and loveable man."

Rosa responded as she walked back into the room,

"With your attitude, I'm wondering for how long?"

The temperature outside was cold, and Derrick stepped out of the car, wearing black leather pants, a black leather jacket, a black turtleneck sweater, and black boots. He was sporting a fresh haircut and a fresh shaven goatee, and black sunglasses. Brother was looking finer than any model that is featured centerfold of a magazine.

Jalesia got up and walked over to open the door before Derrick could knock. Her voice was full of enthusiasm. She greeted Derrick with a kiss on the lips and a hug,

"Good-afternoon, my soon to be husband."

Derrick responded forcing a smile,

"Good-afternoon."

Derrick looked over at Rosa and smiled, and suddenly the smile dropped,

"Good-afternoon mother. I'm sorry, but can I have a word with your daughter?"

Rosa stood up to walk out of the room. She was sensing that Derrick was upset. Rosa answered,

"You sure could have a word. I was hoping you have two or three words."

Derrick grabbed Jalesia by the arm and helped her to sit down. He spoke with a firm, stern voice,

"Come on let's sit down and talk."

Jalesia rolled her eyes and yelled,

"What is your problem? How dare you come in here, and grab on me like that. Have you lost you mind?"

Jalesia got up from the sofa and stomped across the room. She plopped down in a chair and folded her arms in front of her. She looked at Derrick from the corner of her eye with her lips pushed out like a spoiled child throwing a tantrum.

Derrick walked over waving his finger as if he was scolding some school child. He spoke through clenched teeth,

"I have bent over backwards for you, and I am not going to continue to allow you to treat me this way. You have been disrespecting me, and treating me like a child. I have to draw the line somewhere, and that will be here and now. You have talked to me like trash, and have ignored me countless times. Today when you hung the phone up in my face, that was all I could take. Jalesia, I am not going to put up with this. If this is how you treat someone you love, it won't be me."

Jalesia started crying. Derrick knelt down beside her and brushed the tears back from her eyes as he continued to talk to her but now in a softer voice,

"I love you, and I would be the last person to intentionally hurt you. I don't want to fight, and this hurts me, but Jalesia I can't allow you to run over me. I am sorry I have to act this way, but you forced me to."

Jalesia's eyes were filled with tears as she took Derrick's hand and held it up to her cheek. She began to weep,

"Derrick, You are right. I have been a little mean lately, and you are not the first person to say that to me. I am sorry. Can you find it in your heart to forgive me? I do love you."

Derrick stood up and took Jalesia by the hand. He gently helped her up from the chair as he pulled her into his arms and gave her a soft kiss on the lips. Jalesia squeezed her eyes shut and hugged Derrick tightly,

"Derrick, I really do love you."

Derrick agreed,

"I really do love you too, my soon to be wife."

Rosa conveniently walked back into the room and said with a smile,

"Are you two still here? You can take that mushy stuff some where else."

Derrick winked his eye at Rosa,

"Thanks Mother for everything. I know and you know what I am talking about. And yes, we are getting ready to leave. I need to go back to the jeweler to replace Jalesia's engagement ring. Would you like to come?"

Rosa squeezed Derrick's hand and said,

"I would love to go, but you two love birds go ahead. I have work I need to do around the house today."

Chapter Twenty-five

*R*osa was cooking and cleaning when the phone rang,
    "Hello."
The deep husky voice on the other end was full of excitement,
"This is Detective Washington. Is Miss Jalesia Brantz home?"
Rosa responded,
    "Detective Washington, this is Jalesia's mother, Rosa Brantz.
Would you like me to have her to call you back, or is it something I
can help you with?"
Detective Washington answered,
    "Yes ma-am, if you would have her to call me, I would greatly
appreciate it. We have apprehended the suspect, and since Jalesia's
rape and assault, several victims have come forward. All the other
victims had been elderly women, so Jalesia did prevent the old lady
from being raped. Have Jalesia to call me, because we will need to
have her to come back to New York to identify the suspect."
    After Rosa hung up the phone, she fell down on the sofa, and
rested the back of her hand on her forehead and thought,
    "Oh my God! My baby was raped, and she didn't tell me. No
wonder why she has been tossing and turning all night. That also
explains why she was in so much pain, and couldn't bear to sit up. He
was probably rough and caused some type of tearing, especially since
this was her first time. I feel sorry for her and all she ever talked about
was how special her honeymoon would be, when she gives her

husband the gift of a virgin wife. Wow! She must be devastated."

Rosa immediately called Derrick's cell phone number. Jalesia answered the phone and her voice was full of excitement,

"Hello Mother, you have got to see my new ring."

Rosa responded trying to sound excited along with Jalesia,

"That is really nice. I am happy for you all over again. Detective Washington called and said you need to call him. They have apprehended the suspect, and they need you to come to New York to identify him."

Jalesia raised her eyebrows,

"Wow! That didn't take as long as I thought it would. I guess Derrick and I will try to fly out next weekend. Zephanie and Michael are suppose to be in town tomorrow, and returning to New York on Saturday. I guess I will call her to see if she and her husband want to spend the night at Derrick's."

Rosa responded,

"Lea, I love you and I just don't want you going back to New York alone, so whatever your plans are, keep me posted so I won't be worried about you."

"Mother, I know you love me, and thanks for always proving it. I will call you later. Bye-bye."

After Jalesia hung up the phone, she turned up the music and reached over with one hand and intertwined her fingers with Derrick's,

"I must say it again, I must be a blessed woman, because my man is great, and about earlier, let's not fight like that again."

Jalesia jokingly said,

"If you ever grab on me like that again, I will tell my father."

When Derrick stopped at the next red light, Jalesia reached over and kissed him on the lips. She then went back to admiring her ring, watching it sparkling and glittering. Derrick interrupted her thoughts,

"You did not tell me, but did they catch the suspect?"

Jalesia had her back towards Derrick as she stared out the side window while the tears began to fall from her eyes,

"Oh, I'm sorry. I had a million thoughts on my mind. Yes, they did catch him, and we need to go to New York so I can identify him."

Derrick reached over and turned Jalesia's face towards him. He could feel her pain and he asked,

"Do you think you can handle this right now? Looking at his face again will not be easy for you. In fact, I don't think it will be easy for me, because I will want to do him some bodily harm with the way I feel right now."

Jalesia turned back towards the window and spoke to Derrick through her tears,

"I would like to get this over with as soon as possible. It may be a little painful, but this is one situation I want to put behind me."

Derrick gently rubbed Jalesia's back, and said with a smile,

"You will have your man with you, so you have nothing to worry about. I will shield and protect you."

Jalesia picked up the phone and called Zephanie,

"Hello."

"Zep, this is Jalesia. Derrick and I would like to extend our home to you and Michael on tomorrow night. Maybe we can spend some time together, so I can discuss those other issues with you."

Zephanie responded with excitement,

"Jalesia that would be nice! Michael and I have not made any hotel reservations, and I would love to come to your home. Have you told Derrick about being rape yet? The story is something big, and it's all in the news. The suspect has been apprehended and has five counts of rape, assault and robbery, unlawful restraints, burglary, and possession of a firearm at the time of a crime. If convicted the offender can be sentenced to thirty-three years in prison without parole. The crazy man had an opportunity to answer some questions, and he was so silly. He said that he never meant to attack the young Christian girl, but she got in the way. He also said he makes no apologies for the old ladies he had raped and assaulted, because he does not like old women. All of this stemmed from an old lady in church one day, she told him he was going to hell. Let me tell you, brother has some serious issues going on up stairs."

Jalesia interrupted, trying to keep Derrick from knowing what they were discussing,

"Zephanie, we can complete this conversation tomorrow, once we get together."

Zephanie spoke back to Jalesia with a stern voice,

"The only thing I want you to do is tell Derrick before you come out to New York. I would hate for him to find out from the media. They have not mentioned your name, but I'm sure Derrick can put two and two together."

Jalesia answered trying to talk between the lines,

"Yes, you are right, but not yet. We will discuss that in more details on tomorrow. Do I need to pick you up from the airport?"

"No, that would not be necessary. Michael and I can rent a vehicle once we get there."

"No, Zephanie, that would not be necessary, you can borrow one of Derrick's cars. With all you have done for me, that would be the least we can do for you. What time is your flight scheduled to arrive? Derrick and I will be there to pick you and Michael up."

Zephanie surrendered,

"Okay, our flight is scheduled to arrive at 9:15 tomorrow morning. I will see you then. Anyhow, let me go. I have patients waiting. Good bye."

"Bye-Bye."

As Derrick pulled into the drive way, he reminded Jalesia that they have counseling in the morning at 10:00, so they may need to back the time up with Pastor Hamilton.

While in the mall Derrick had bought some more video games for his X-box and his Play Station 2 game systems. Derrick was getting bags out of the car while Jalesia went inside. He brought all the bags into the family room. When Derrick walked in he held Jalesia in his arms for a few minutes. Jalesia starred into Derrick's eyes, and wanted desperately to tell him about the rape incident, but she could not muster up the nerves.

Derrick's form of entertainment that evening would be to sit in front of the 62-inch, flat screen T.V. and play video games.

After Jalesia and Derrick got dressed comfortably for bed, they met up in the family room.

Derrick did not know Jalesia knew how to play video games, and as soon as he kicked the ball off to Jalesia, she was running the ball back for a touchdown. Derrick put the game on pause, and stood up,

"Whoa! Wait a minute. That's not fair. Where did you learn how to play? I can't let you beat me."

Jalesia was laughing at the intense look on Derrick's face, and she pulled him back down to the floor,

"Release the button so I can score this touchdown. Remember, being a Christian has its advantages in the real world too. Since I don't hang out at clubs all the time, and I don't do krunk parties, I get together with some friends and we play video games, spades, or bid wiz."

Derrick lifted up his hand for a high five,

"I did not know you were a spade player. Do you play, or are you a player?"

Jalesia responded as she stood up and twirled around,

"I am a real player, but we can discuss that after I spank your butt in this football game. So come on back down here and let's get it on."

Derrick put on his game face, as he picked up his controller, and motioned for Jalesia to bring it on,

"There is no way I will let you beat me in this football game, or any game."

Jalesia was up for the challenge. She looked at Derrick and saw that he had an intense look on his face as if he did not want to loose the football game.

Jalesia replied,

"I knew from the first day I met you, that you were cocky, but talk is cheap. I know you are confident, and that's why I love you so."

Jalesia leaned over and kissed Derrick softly on the lips. He remembered how nice it was kissing Jalesia. He then leaned over and kissed Jalesia softly. Derrick starred into Jalesia's eyes. He moved closer to Jalesia and pulled her into his arms and gave her a long hot kiss.

Jalesia changed the mood, when she sat up and said,

"Okay, let's get back to the video game."

The very next play Derrick had the ball running it back for a touchdown. Derrick was up, dancing around the room, and talking trash. Jalesia was happy to see Derrick have so much fun.

They continued to play different games all night, football, basketball, fight games, and mission games. Jalesia was tired, and ready to turn in,

"Derrick I believe you could play this game all night, but I am tired, and ready to go to bed."

Derrick stood up and reached for Jalesia's hand and helped her up off the floor. When Jalesia stood to her feet, she put her arms around Derrick's neck, and Jalesia spoke softly,

"Soon we will be free to do, and act like we want to with one another."

Derrick interjected, smiling,

"Yes, you are right, soon I will not have to leave out of the bedroom while you change clothes. After you are officially Mrs. Dubois, if it gets so hot in the room that the walls catch on fire, it will be our business."

Jalesia hugged Derrick tightly, as she stroked him in his back,

"Sweetheart, I really do love you, and I have a lot on my mind that I have to deal with. There is something I need to tell you, but now is not the time."

Derrick gently lifted Jalesia's chin, and looked deeply into her eyes again. This time Jalesia's eyes were filled with tears as she took a deep breath and began to cry,

"Derrick, I don't ever want to loose you. I feel like you are a missing piece in my life. I am afraid. I am confused. I am worried, and I have so many different mixed feelings that I can't explain."

Derrick held Jalesia in his arms,

"Shhhhh! You don't ever have to worry about loosing me. I wish we didn't have to wait these next four months to be married. I wish we could make it official tomorrow when we talk with Pastor Hamilton—." Derrick stopped in the middle of his thought and snapped his finger, "Sweetheart, we forgot to call Pastor Hamilton about our counseling on tomorrow, and we're suppose to pick Michael and Zephanie up from the airport."

Jalesia kissed Derrick softly and assured him that she has everything under control.

"Don't worry, I will call Pastor Hamilton now and push back the time for us to meet with him."

Jalesia yawned deeply and stretched long and hard, then said in a sleepy voice,

"We still need to get up early, so I guess we better try to get some rest."

They lightly kissed one another, and said goodnight. Jalesia went to the Master bedroom, and Derrick went to the master guest suite. The master guest suite was all the way on the other side of the house. After Jalesia brushed her teeth, and wrapped her hair, she walked over to the other side of the house where Derrick was standing in the mirror, in the bathroom with no shirt, and his boxer shorts, brushing his teeth. When she walked in, she startled Derrick because he jumped,

"I'm sorry, I did not mean to startle you."

Derrick responded,

"That's not a problem. Are you okay?"

Derrick walked out of the bathroom, and went into the bedroom and put on his red satin pajamas. Jalesia continued to watch Derrick get dressed for bed,

"Derrick, have I told you lately that I love you?"

Derrick walked up to Jalesia, and turned her towards the door, and playfully pushed her out of the room,

"Yes you have, and I love you too. But why are you up in here trying to start something?"

Jalesia was in a playful mood as she playfully grabbed Derrick's butt, then ran out of the room and yelled back,

"Good-night sweetheart, I love you."

Derrick yelled back,

"I love you too."

Jalesia walked back into her bedroom and removed the designer pillows from her bed, and got under the covers. As soon as she found a comfortable spot, Derrick walked into the room and extended forth his hand to Jalesia and said,

"Sweetheart, would you come and join me?"

Jalesia put her hand in Derrick's hand and spoke softly,

"Sure, what is it that you want?"

Derrick took two jumbo downy pillows out of the closet and put them on the floor next to the bed. He then knelt down on one of the pillows, and helped Jalesia down on her knees. Derrick spoke sincerely,

"I want you to join me for prayer. I feel if we start off right, we will end up right."

Jalesia already had her head bowed, and her fingers interlocked, ready for Derrick to start praying. Derrick spoke softly,

"I feel a need to pray tonight, because I am really concern about you. Can we hold hands as I pray?"

Jalesia did not exchange a word with Derrick, but interlocked her hand with his hand, closed her eyes, and Derrick prayed a sincere prayer.

After prayer Jalesia stood up and was crying. When Derrick stood, he too had been crying. Derrick wrapped his arms around Jalesia, and spoke softly,

"I know God is able to help you, and I want you to know, He said everything will be alright. I am going to say goodnight, so you can get your rest. We have a full day ahead of us on tomorrow."

Chapter Twenty-six

*E*very time Jalesia found herself settling, she would see the rapist face, and think about how painful things were for her.

Jalesia picked up the phone to call the best friend she has.

The phone rang,

"Hello."

The voice on the other end was very hoarse.

"Mother, it's me. I need to talk with you."

Rosa sat up in bed and reached to the foot of the bed for her robe,

"Baby hold on for a minute. I need to go in the other room, because your father is snoring out of control."

Once Rosa went into the living room, she sat on the sofa with her legs underneath her. She turned the lamp on and cleared the cobwebs out of her head as her eyes adjusted to the dim light.

Rosa spoke softly,

"Are you okay? It sounds like something is wrong."

Jalesia responded in a whisper,

"Mother, I omitted to tell you the complete story as to what happened to me in New York. The man that assaulted me also raped me."

Rosa sighed deeply,

"Oh my God! I thought there was more. Why didn't you tell me?"

Jalesia continued,

"Mother, this has been the hardest thing for me to deal with, because I don't want to loose Derrick. I am afraid if I tell him, he will not want to be with me anymore. I figure if we get married, he would have a better chance of staying with me."

Rosa whispered back,

"Baby, that is deception. You have a better chance if you were open and up front with him. I know you don't want to loose him, but that is his choice. I am not taking sides, because you are my child, but I also have to tell you what's right. Sweetheart, the issue is not that you were raped, the issue is keeping this from Derrick. That is your decision to make, but if you want the truth from me, it would be better if you were open and honest with Derrick. Enough of that." Rosa said changing the subject. "Now I want to know how are you doing, physically and emotionally. You may need to see a doctor about your roller coaster of emotions."

Jalesia began to cry,

"Mother, what ever you do, don't tell Derrick, let me tell him. Zephanie has been great through all of this. She will be here tomorrow, and she will counsel me. Mother this ordeal has really hurt me emotionally, and I am constantly praying, asking God to help me. The physical part is almost over. I am healing really well. I was torn and had to get some stitches. Also, I have been on antibiotic for the irritation to the cervix that caused some minor bleeding. Dr. Morris, Zephanie, will remove the stitches tomorrow."

Rosa tilted her head back and bit down on her lip,

"Lea, I am here for you. I want what is best for you, but I think you will go wrong if you do not tell Derrick the whole story. The two of you will be going to New York, and if he finds out from someone else, it could be devastating if the woman he loves has deceived him. Take a walk in Derrick's shoes. How would you feel if something of this magnitude was withheld from you? And the one person that loves you the most knew about it, but did not tell you. Baby, reevaluate the situation, and let him know. Think of it this way, I would rather someone leave me because I was honest, than for some one to leave because I was deceptive."

Jalesia was still crying,

"Mother, you are making this hard for me, but continue to pray for me. I'll sleep on it tonight, and allow the Lord to lead me and..."

Rosa interrupted,

"Lea, I love you, and no matter what decision you make, I am here for you. I just hate that you are force to have to make this decision at all. The man that interrupted your life, I hope God fix him. Sweetie, I know you will make the right decision. I stand behind you, and I know everything will be all right. I will keep you in my prayers, because we know that Jesus knows how to fix it. I love you and give my handsome, soon to be son-in-law a hug and kiss for me. I am going to say goodnight, because I want you to get your rest."

Jalesia responded,

"Thanks Mother, I love you too. Goodnight"

Chapter Twenty-seven

*J*alesia had a rough night sleeping. She tossed and turned all night, and she kicked and fought in her sleep as well. Jalesia could see the sunlight through her eyelids. Then, she slowly opened her eyes, and adjusted to the morning sun. This was Jalesia first morning waking up in Derrick's master suite; therefore, her eyes had to adjust to the new surroundings. As Jalesia stretched and kicked from under the covers, she looked around the room. Derrick was asleep on the burgundy chaise next to the bed. When he heard Jalesia waking up, he opened his eyes.

Jalesia asked, in a hoarse morning voice,

"What are you doing in here?"

Derrick sat up and slipped on his bedroom shoes. He walked over to Jalesia's bed and put his arm around her waist. He lightly kissed her on the lips. Jalesia pulled away and said,

"I have not brushed my teeth this morning, and here you are over here kissing on me."

Derrick was in a playful mood. He grabbed Jalesia again and licked her lips with his tongue. Jalesia pushed him away laughing,

"Uuuuuugh!!!!!! Derrick, would you stop. Do you always wake up in a playful mood? If you do, I'll have to sleep in another room once we get married. I told you, I have not had a chance to brush my teeth."

Derrick responded,

"You need to get used to it, because we have a few months before we're married. You have to be out of your mind, if I wake up in a romantic mood and I have to wait until you brush your teeth, or until I brush my teeth, before I can kiss you."

Derrick was still playing as he pulled Jalesia's silk scarf off her head and said,

"Do I have to wait until you run over to the vanity and comb your hair before I can look at you? Yes, I am definitely a morning person. I love playing in the morning, and once we are married, I hope to be doing a lot more than playing."

Jalesia playfully slapped Derrick's arm and reached for her scarf,

"Give me back my scarf. Too bad you don't have anything I can pull off you. Why are you bothering me anyway? It's 6:00 in the morning and we both need our rest."

Derrick was still playing keep-away with the scarf, but his voice shifted to a more serious tone as he wrapped the scarf around his neck and said,

"Are you rested this morning, because I am going to need to get you some help with sleeping. I came in here because I heard you screaming help in your sleep. But when I walked in the room you were sound asleep. During the night you were kicking and fighting, but your only words were stop and please. I figured this was due to your experience with the attacker."

Jalesia squeezed Derrick's hand, and said,

"I hope when I have counseling with Zephanie on tomorrow, she can help me to start moving on with my life."

Jalesia was trying to get out of bed, but Derrick was still playing. He was holding her down and would not let her get up. Jalesia spoke with an urgent voice,

"Derrick, please move. It is obvious you don't understand the importance of needing to go to the bathroom once you wake up in the morning."

Chapter Twenty-eight

Zephanie and Michael were the forth and fifth persons off the plane. When Jalesia saw Zephanie she ran over to give her a big hug. Zephanie was wearing her long, thick, healthy, black hair down at shoulder length. She had on a dark brown pants suit, with a pair of dark brown, suede pumps.

Michael's complexion was medium brown. He was sporting a light full beard with a nicely trimmed afro. Michael was wearing a pair of dark brown slacks with a beige and brown sports coat.

Zephanie took Jalesia by the hand,

"Come on, let me introduce you to Michael, and I certainly want to meet Derrick."

Zephanie reached up and brushed Jalesia's hair back, "Look at you. You have healed well from the scratches and black eyes. You're really looking nice. Zephanie kept touching Jalesia, and looking and smiling, "Jalesia, please forgive me for looking so hard, but I am amazed at how beautiful you are. I guess meeting you in the hospital was a shock, because seeing you now is like seeing someone totally different."

Zephanie reached for Michael's hand, "Jalesia this is Michael, my wonderful husband, and Michael this is Jalesia." Michael extended out his arms and they greeted one another with a hug.

Jalesia was smiling from ear to ear, and she took Derrick by the hand,

"Zephanie and Michael, this is Derrick, my soon to be husband, and Derrick this is Zephanie and Michael."

Zephanie hugged Derrick and kissed him on the cheek. Michael and Derrick gave each other an open hug.

Derrick asked,

"Should we pick up your luggage, so we can get out of here and head home?"

Michael responded,

"I can agree to that."

Jalesia and Zephanie were walking ahead of Michael and Derrick. Zephanie had her arm around Jalesia's waist. She was surprised how well Jalesia had recovered.

"I can't believe how beautiful you are."

Jalesia was laughing, and thanking Zephanie for the compliment. She then said,

"I must have looked like a monster in the hospital room. I remembered you telling me that I did not look bad."

Zephanie laughed back at Jalesia's remark,

"Girl, I am so glad I had never seen you before, because seeing you now, I would have lied to you in the hospital room. Girl, you really did look bad."

Jalesia changed the subject,

"Are you all hungry? Do you want to grab some breakfast?"

"No, I am fine. Maybe we can do lunch or dinner later. Michael and I have so much to do today. We may need to spend a few days with you, if you don't mind. We thought we were leaving Sunday morning, but it's going to take some time to get the house situation completed."

Jalesia and Zephanie continued to walk closely together as if they were life long friends that had not seen one another for a while. They were walking so fast through the airport that they were well ahead of Michael and Derrick.

Jalesia said,

"You can stay as long as you need to. The more time we have together, the better. Derrick and I have our Marriage Counseling Session today with Pastor Hamilton, and he is not at all pleased to be doing this. He tells me that he already knows how to treat me, with honor and respect. Also he says that he does not need a counselor telling him how to abstain."

Zephanie stopped walking for a minute, and took Jalesia by the hand,

"Girl, that is beautiful. When Michael and I were engaged we were both Christians, but we did not wait. I could have kicked my own butt because we almost made it. One night Michael lit a match and the flames kindled, and I could not put out the fire, not until everything had burned up. We ended up yielding to our burning desires. Thank God for his grace and mercy. I often ask myself, what if I did not enjoy Michael, or he did not enjoy me. Would we still be together? I would tell anyone not to take that chance but to wait, hold on, and be strong in the Lord."

Derrick and Michael sat in the front seat of the Bentley, and Jalesia and Zephanie sat in the back. Derrick's house was approximately fifteen minutes from the airport. When they arrived at the house, Michael and Derrick were laughing and talking as if they had known one another for years. Zephanie took her purse out of the car and left her luggage for Michael and Derrick to bring into the house.

Once inside the house, Jalesia escorted Zephanie to the guest suite, where she and Michael would occupy while they were there.

Maria, the maid, was preparing to leave for the day. The house was immaculate. Maria left candles lit, and the fragrance from the scented candles lingered in the air. The temperature was still a little nippy for Florida weather. Spring was only a few days away.

Derrick took Michael on a tour around the house and showed him all of his vehicles. Michael was impressed to see the many cars Derrick had parked in his garage. They stopped by the basketball court and they were standing out talking. This was Zephanie's opportunity to talk briefly with Jalesia. Zephanie sat on the sofa and crossed her legs in front of her. Jalesia sat facing Zephanie as she pulled her legs underneath her. Zephanie reached over and gently placed her hand on top of Jalesia's hand.

Zephanie starred at Jalesia with eyes full of immense concern. Jalesia would not give Zephanie eye contact. Zephanie knelt down in front of Jalesia. She pulled Jalesia into her arms and began to rock her,

"Don't worry Jalesia, it going to be alright. We don't have to talk now if you don't want to. I see your hurt, I feel your hurt, and I am going to help you rid your hurt."

Jalesia hugged Zephanie back,

"Don't make me cry. I want to be able to go to counseling today without that horrible incident on my mind."

Zephanie pulled away and looked into Jalesia's eyes again,

"Jalesia, I know exactly how you feel, and the devil is a liar. I am here for you, and with God on your side, He will help us through this. Remember what the scripture says in Romans 8:32, *If God be for us who can be against us.*"

Jalesia extended both of her hands to Zephanie and said,

"How can I say thank you. I know our friendship is of the Lord."

Zephanie interrupted and put her hands up to her mouth,

"Oh my God!! Oh – My - God!!"

Jalesia turned and looked behind her trying to see why Zephanie was screaming. By this time Michael and Derrick were walking into the house. Zephanie was waving for Michael to come over where she was,

"Mike, Come here. You have got to see this!"

Zephanie picked up Jalesia's hand and said,

"Michael, that is the ring that you have been saving to get me. I could give you the complete description: heart shape cut, F color, approx 3.5 carats, set in a six prong platinum braded band. Tell me, I know I am right. The value is 56k, right?"

Michael nodded his head in agreement as he spoke with enthusiasm,

"Derrick, Zephanie is right. I promised her I would have that ring for her on our fifth wedding anniversary coming up in May. She and I both said we would not find anyone else with that ring, and low and behold, you have it."

Jalesia was smiling as she held her hand up flashing the ring. Derrick responded,

"Zephanie, You are pretty good. You are exactly right. I guess two great minds think alike. The jeweler promised me that I would not see anyone else with that ring. It's amazing how you guessed the description of the ring."

Jalesia was humble as she replied,

"I did not pick out this ring. It was all Derrick's doing. I have never owned a diamond before I met Derrick. I did not know there was a specialist in a jewelry store, a certified gemologist. All this stuff is new to me. I'm just a down home girl, and you will never see me trying to be something I am not. God has been too good to me, for me to forget where I came from."

Derrick walked over behind Jalesia and put his hands on her shoulders. He lightly massaged her shoulders, and with a smile said,

"This is why I love this woman so much, because she is real."

Derrick looked down at his watch and quickly said,

"Michael, Jalesia and I have to be heading to counseling this morning, but you have the keys to the house and to the Lincoln. Now if you want to drive the Vanquish or the Hummer, the keys are hanging by the garage door."

Jalesia stood up,

"I guess Derrick is right. We need to leave now if we are going to make it to counseling on time. And please don't forget we are going to this black-owned seafood restaurant tonight. I want to share with you how Derrick and I met, and where he took me on our first date."

Chapter Twenty-nine

*P*astor Hamilton was a tall dark skinned man on the fat side. He was a young pastor, but full of the anointing and wisdom.

When Jalesia and Derrick walked into the Pastor's study, Pastor Hamilton extended his hand towards the two leather chairs opposite his mahogany desk. Pastor Hamilton was wearing a long sleeve shirt and a tie with praying hands on it.

Jalesia introduced Derrick,

"Pastor, this is my fiancé, Derrick, and Derrick, this is Pastor Hamilton."

They greeted one another with a firm handshake. For the first time, Jalesia could see that Derrick was nervous. He was shaking his legs and twiddling his thumbs as he held his head down.

Pastor Hamilton was a soft-spoken man, and he began the conversation,

"Don't be nervous in the service, before we began we are going to pray."

Pastor prayed and proceeded to explain the course of the morning. He looked over at Derrick,

"Are you sure you are going to be alright? Man, you are looking like you're about to pass out. Does my daughter have a gun drawn on you?"

Derrick looked up at Pastor Hamilton and smiled,

No, she does not. I am really looking forward to the day when this lady will be my wife. It is almost scary how much I love her. I believe that is why I am so nervous, because I have never loved anyone this way. I am sure there is a lot of things I still don't know, but I am willing to stay, and learn all I can. We are not having sex; therefore I know it is not a physical thing. This is real love."

Pastor Hamilton waved at Derrick,

"Keep talking man, you are making my job really easy. It's like you really don't need counseling, because you already know what we we're going to discuss."

Pastor Hamilton leaned back in his chair with his finger inter-locked behind his head and his feet propped up on the shinny mahogany desk. He took a deep breath and said,

"It's good to love like that, because I didn't love my wife that deeply until after we were married. Have you all decided what church you would be attending after you're married?"

Derrick answered,

"We never really discussed that, because I know Jalesia would follow me any where I go."

Jalesia was shaking her head in agreement, because she knew if she allowed Derrick the control, she would get to make the decision,

"Yes sir Pastor, Derrick is correct. We have never discussed that, but he will soon be my husband, and I trust every decision he makes. I would follow him to any church he would be comfortable in."

Pastor Hamilton sat up in his seat. His eyebrows curled up as his forehead wrinkled,

"You mean to tell me that there is a possibility that my daughter will be leaving me?"

Derrick smiled back at Pastor Hamilton and said,

"Don't get nervous in the service, is that what somebody told me? Initially, we will become members of this church, but I believe my soon to be wife is going to pursue her calling in ministry. She may want to start her own mission. We have discussed that, so I want you and this organization to know if she is led to get started, I support her one hundred percent."

Pastor Hamilton turned around in his chair and said,

"Listen here Doc, I knew that she was called in ministry before you did. I never hold any one back, and I will help her in any way that I can. This church knows how to work with women in ministry."

Pastor Hamilton continued discussing marriage and commitment, obedience and sacrifice, and how Derrick and Jalesia will be no more two, but will become as one. When Pastor Hamilton finished discussing all the ups and downs, the ends and outs, he then asked,

"Now, are you both willing to sacrifice of yourselves to commit to one another?"

Derrick eyes gleamed as he took Jalesia by the hand and spoke softly,

"I am willing to sacrifice everything for this lady."

Pastor Hamilton looked at Jalesia, and she said,

"I am willing to commit totally to Mr. Derrick Dubois."

Pastor Hamilton then stood up and pulled his pants over his stomach. He leaned forward over his desk and anointed Derrick and Jalesia's head with oil,

"You two don't need any more marriage sessions, but I would like to get together again. We need to discuss the church doctrine, so Derrick can understand what we believe in this church."

Jalesia reminded Pastor Hamilton that they would be going to New York next weekend, and to keep them in his prayers. Pastor Hamilton prayed for Jalesia's strength to endure the test she has at hand. He also prayed for a long successful marriage for Derrick and Jalesia.

Chapter Thirty

*D*errick and Jalesia were home stretch out on the sofa. Jalesia was lying in front of Derrick asleep. Derrick had his arm around Jalesia with the remote control in hand while he was trying to find something of interest to watch on television.

When Michael and Zephanie walked through the door, it was approximately three-thirty, and Jalesia did not hear them when they came through the door. She was sound asleep. Zephanie walked over to the sofa and placed one finger over her lips, motioning to Derrick to please be quiet.

Zephanie then knelt down on the floor in front of Jalesia. She playfully pinched Jalesia's nose close and then let go. There was no response from Jalesia; therefore, Zephanie pinched her nose again. This time Jalesia knocked her hand out of the way and said,

"Stop Derrick."

Zephanie continued to pinch her nose. The creases in Jalesia's forehead showed that she was getting frustrated. Jalesia took a deep breath and said,

"Sweetheart, please stop! You play entirely too much. Let me get just a few more minutes of rest, and I will wake up as soon as Michael and Zephanie get here."

While Jalesia was talking, Zephanie put her hand over Jalesia's mouth. With a frown on her face, Jalesia grabbed Zephanie's hand and opened her eyes. After she opened her eyes and realized it was

Zephanie, Jalesia smiled, sat up and said,

"Girl, you should not play like that. You were about to make my man get in trouble, because Derrick also loves to play like that."

Zephanie answered,

"I should be the last one to play like that because Michael does it all the time. I know how aggravating that can be."

Zephanie stood to her feet and snapped her finger,

"So, did you and Derrick eat?"

Derrick stood up and gathered himself together, and told Michael to come go with him outside. They waited for Jalesia and Zephanie at the car. After Michael and Derrick left out of the house, Zephanie and Jalesia had some private time together. Jalesia was in the bathroom mirror refreshing her make up when Zephanie walked in the room. Zephanie asked,

"Did your sutures come out? I tried to put them in so you would be able to remove them once you're healed."

Jalesia answered,

"Yes, in fact I was able to remove them today. It did hurt a little because you put a knot in one end."

Zephanie raised her eyebrow as she watched Jalesia put on her make up,

"So, when are you going to tell Derrick? You really need to know how important it is for him to know. Your wedding date is not far off, and on your honeymoon, Derrick will be looking forward to making love to you. The first time you make love after you have been raped, could be a nightmare. This is not something someone told me, but I know this first hand. I thank God I told Michael, because he knew how to be gentle and considerate of what I had gone through."

Jalesia leaned back on the counter top and began to cry,

"I want to tell Derrick, but I am afraid of how he will handle it. Derrick thinks he's marrying this virgin, someone who has saved herself for him. But in all actuality he's, marrying a rape victim." Jalesia became angry and continued, " He is marrying someone who has been ripped, stretched, and torn."

Zephanie put her arms around Jalesia and said,

"J, meet me in the family room, and let me go outside and ask the men to give us an hour to talk."

Zephanie walked outside where Derrick and Michael were standing,

"Derrick, Jalesia and I will be a while. I need to have a few minutes with her as a friend. Will the two of you hang out for about an hour, and when you return, we can go out to dinner."

Derrick asked with a concerned tone,

"Is she alright? Should I stay to go through the counseling with her? I promised her I would not leave her anymore."

"Derrick, she's going to be okay. Please, let me have about an hour alone so we can deal with some issues. This is not a counseling session, I just want to talk with her as a friend."

"Zephanie, I am concern about her sleeping at night. She screams, kicks, and fights in her sleep. Her mom told me that she also cries in her sleep. Whatever it takes to make it better for her, let's do it."

"Derrick, if you don't mind, I am going to sleep in the room with her tonight, so I can monitor her. I am sure after we talk today, she will be able to sleep again."

Derrick walked in the house with Zephanie, and knelt down on the floor where Jalesia was sitting,

"Are you okay? I told Zephanie if you did not want me to leave, I would stay here with you."

Jalesia answered,

"No Derrick, you can go. Zephanie and I have a lot to talk about. I will be all right. You and Michael go and have a good time."

Jalesia took the back of her hand and lovingly glided it down the side of Derrick's face as she spoke softly,

"Have I told you lately that I love you?"

Derrick answered,

"You just did, and I love you too."

Derrick rested his forehead on Jalesia's forehead. He then softly kissed her.

After Derrick and Michael left, Jalesia sat on the sofa, and Zephanie went to the bathroom. She came back with some face towels in a basin with warm water. Zephanie pulled the leather chair next to the sofa, and asked Jalesia to stretch out on the sofa with her feet up.

Zephanie placed two pillows under Jalesia's feet. She explained to Jalesia that she was going to ask some questions that would be painful, but she would not act on her emotions. Zephanie had her pad and pen in her hand, and she led out with a spirit-filled prayer. Zephanie started with the first question,

"J, what are you afraid of?"

Jalesia tried to get totally relaxed as she closed her eyes and responded,

"First of all, I don't want to loose Derrick. It has nothing to do with his money, but I really do love him. You know this is strange, but I don't desire Derrick like I used to. When I look at Derrick, you can tell Derrick is a man that is well endowed, or should I say packing a trunk. I don't know if I will be able to handle him. I am really afraid of having sex with him. I talk trash to him like I can't wait, but the closer I get to my wedding day, the more frighten I become. When I think about that rapist, and he was not nearly as developed as Derrick, and if the rapist ripped and tore me, I wonder how bad is this going to hurt with Derrick."

Zephanie was writing while Jalesia was talking. Jalesia shifted in her seat, and the room grew silent for a few moments, and then she continued.

"At night I can hear that man moaning and groaning in my ear. I have never hated anyone, and I know how final death is, but I wish that man was dead." Jalesia started crying. "I really do wish the man was dead. He came into my life and disrupted my happiness. I can never go back to being a virgin. I can't begin to tell you how important my virginity was to me. All throughout high school and college, all of my girlfriends would tell me about good sex and bad sex. I turned away every opportunity I had, and I had to sit back and listen to my girlfriends tell me, 'girl, you don't know what you're missing' and along comes this butt hole to interrupt my life."

Jalesia began to cry harder, and Zephanie picked up one of the warm towels and wiped Jalesia's face.

"Let it all out, cry and scream as loud as you want to, but release it. Tell me everything."

Jalesia took a deep breath and continued,

"I think about that night when I asked Derrick, the man I know I love with all my heart, to make love to me. He told me he would wait, because he wanted my first time to be special. Derrick promised me then, that my first time would be a day I will always remember. Then this bastard comes in and steals the one thing I treasured, out side of spiritual things, and that is my virginity."

Jalesia sat up on the sofa and placed one of the sofa pillows in her lap. She buried her face in the pillow and cried out of control. While hitting and squeezing the pillow, she cried out,

"I've asked myself, where was God, and why would He allow this to happen to me? Don't get me wrong, I know I need the Lord in my life, and I know how important He is in my life. I just can't understand why He would allow this to happen. My thoughts have been, why did this have to happen? I cherished the fact of being a Christian, and being a virgin."

Jalesia dropped to her knees and lifted up her hands in the air as the tears continued to flow,

"W-H-Y??? W-H-Y??? OH GOD! I don't understand. Lord Please, help me understand."

When Zephanie saw that Jalesia was pouring out all of her emotions, she place one hand on Jalesia's back and gently stroked downward,

"It's okay. Let it all out. This is the only way to deal with it. Release it all, there is no one here but you and I."

Zephanie sat on the sofa as Jalesia was kneeling on the floor. Zephanie gently pulled Jalesia's head in her lap, and wiped her tears away. Jalesia began to take deep quivery breaths as she gradually began to calm down. She squeezed her eyes shut as she continued to talk,

"You know, I would also like to get the cab driver, because if it was not for him, I would have never been in those projects. The cab driver was the first one to disrupt my life when he robbed me. Do we just let him go free? I would like to see both of those men punished."

Once Jalesia finished, Zephanie wiped her face with one of the warm face towels, and helped Jalesia back up on the sofa. Zephanie sat back in the chair across from Jalesia.

She looked at Jalesia and said,

"Jalesia, first thing, Derrick really does love you, and you don't stand a chance of loosing him. The only way I can see that happening is through deception. You must find a way to tell Derrick. If you feel waiting is better, then that is up to you. Derrick's love making to you will be a lot sweeter if he knows what he is up against. This is a decision only you can make, but I think you should tell him now."

Zephanie started smiling, as she lifted her hand for a high five,

"Secondly, I have to give it to you. Girl, your man is definitely fine. I believe he could be well endowed, but you will be able to handle him. That's how our bodies are made. You will be fine. Understand, that you were not torn because that negro was big, but he didn't care about what he was doing. He forced himself on you. You can never compare rape to love, no matter how you look at it. A man that loves you will know how to put it on you right. He will handle you with kit gloves, and the love will be sweet."

Jalesia sat up as she listened attentively, as Zephanie continued,

"You asked how could you allow yourself, being a Christian, to get into compromising positions of coming close to making love to Derrick. When you are alone with someone you love, and they love you equally in return, and if you are hugging and kissing, holding and rubbing one another, it is highly possible to come close. I'm surprised that both of you were able to stop. I understand that we are Christians, and I also know that we are humans. Indeed the spirit is willing, but the flesh is weak. I make no excuses for Michael and I, but I told you he lit the match, and it was impossible for me to put out the fire. I just thank God for his grace and mercy, but two years after we were married, I was raped coming home from work. Someone was there for me, and I promised the Lord that I would be a blessing to someone else one day.

I know you said you no longer desire Derrick, but give it some time and I'm confident your feelings will change. Making love is not something dirty. Your thoughts are still on the pain that you experienced. Being with Derrick is not going to be like that. After you have gotten married, you will be able to explore many options, and I promise you, it will not be nasty.

After today you will not be hearing the moans and groans any more. You had to release a lot of emotions today in order to move on. Next weekend when you go to New York, you will definitely find some closure.

Sometimes we act and say things out of anger. The thoughts you had about the rapist was okay, because of the horrible things he had done. Now you have to forgive, and ask God to help you to move on.

I understand how important your virginity was, but Jalesia you can't go back and undo what has been done. This is where you must turn it over to the Lord, and let Him work it out. The rapist and the cab driver will wish you were the one that punish them, after they get what God has for them."

Jalesia interrupted as she smiled at Zephanie,

"I can't believe I'm starting to feel better already."

Zephanie continued,

"One more thing I need to address, and this is on the spiritual tip. You said you don't see God, but He is all up in there. The cab driver had a knife, the rapist had a gun, you starred down the barrel of the gun, the gun was put in your mouth, but did I hear you ask where was God? You did not get any transmitted diseases, you did not get AIDS, and you did not get pregnant. You have completely healed, but again, did I hear you ask where was God?"

Jalesia concluded,

"I got the picture. God was there all the time. We don't always understand, but I know the big picture is, '*All things work together for the good to them that love God, to them who are the call according to His purpose.*' The Bible did not say all things are good, but it does say that all things are working for my good."

Zephanie added,

"You have a testimony that will help women and men around the world. Being in ministry, you don't know how many people will come to you with this problem, and you can help them from first hand experience. Don't look at the negative, but always find the positive, and that is where you will see God."

Jalesia got up and walked over to Zephanie and hugged her tightly,

"Zephanie thanks for everything. You have truly been a blessing to me. How can I ever repay you?"

"What are friends for? We don't repay, we just be there for one another."

Chapter Thirty-one

*W*hen Derrick and Jalesia arrive in New York, they took care of business early. Jalesia identified the suspect. The process did not take long, because the detectives knew they had the right man. Derrick was a little disappointed, because Jalesia did not involve him when she met with the detectives. Derrick felt that he was left out. Jalesia had been able to keep Derrick from hearing about the rape incident all day.

The celebration dinner was going to be at Derrick's restaurant. While Derrick and Jalesia were at the apartment complex, Zephanie came over for Jalesia to put her hair in an up style. Zephanie was surprised, for as long as they lived in New York, they had never been to Derrick's restaurant. Zephanie could not believe she would have ever met the owner of that upscale restaurant.

While Zephanie and Jalesia were talking, Derrick came back into the room,

"Sweetheart, you and Zephanie need to stop talking so much so you can get dressed for dinner. I have ran you bath water, so you need to get into the tub before your water gets cold."

Zephanie answered,

"I guess Derrick is right. I'll get my things, and head home so I can get dressed."

Jalesia went into the bathroom, closed the door and turned on some gospel music. While in the living room, Derrick turned on the television. The announcer was getting ready for a commercial break, and they showed a picture of the man that had assaulted Jalesia. The announcer said, "When we return from break the long awaited story of this man who has finally been identified. You don't want to miss this story when we return."

Derrick pointed towards the television as his face wrinkled. He frowned and said,

"I've got to hear this story. That bastard is lucky he's not a dead man, because if I could get my hands on him, he would not be smiling in front of the camera like that."

Zephanie tried to prevent Derrick from seeing the news. She knew if Derrick saw this story, he would be angry. She walked in front of the television and turned the power off and said,

"Derrick, would you walk me out, I want to get dressed so we can have some fun tonight."

Derrick stood up and walked towards his bedroom,

"Zephanie, I would love to walk you out, but I'm going in my room and lock my door, because it is a must that I see this story."

Zephanie tried to make it to the door before Derrick locked the door. She knocked on the door, and shouted through the door trying to get Derrick to open it, but Derrick turned the volume up on the television to drown out Zephanie's sound.

The news anchor came back with the story, and Zephanie was still standing at the door knocking,

"Please Derrick, you don't want to do this. Open the door. Derrick, please let me explain."

Five minutes later, Derrick walked to the door and opened it. Zephanie was standing there, and Derrick's face was pale. He was extremely angry.

Zephanie spoke as her voice trembled. She reached for Derrick's hand, and he snatched away, as he felled back on the doorpost. Zephanie began to plead with Derrick,

"Derrick, you told me to help Jalesia, and I have been trying to help her through this difficult situation. She's gone through a lot, so please, don't be angry."

Derrick rolled his eyes at Zephanie, as he spoke through clenched teeth,

"Angry? No, I'm not angry. I am hurt. How can I marry a woman that can't be honest with me? A woman who would lie, cover up, cheat, deceive, and betray me!"

Derrick turned his back to Zephanie to keep her from seeing his tears. She reached for Derrick as she rubbed him in his back. She softly spoke,

"Derrick, please let me explain...."

Derrick abruptly interrupted as he held up his hand to stop Zephanie from speaking,

"No, don't explain anything! You didn't explain before now. I don't want to hear it."

Derrick wiped away his tears and continued speaking to Zephanie in anger,

"I tell you what, don't say a word to Jalesia, because if you let on that I know, you will be the one to marry her. I just want to see how long will she deceive me. I want to know what kind of woman she is. I have poured out everything to her, and she would withhold something this important from me!"

Derrick tapped in his chest with his hand as he paced back and forth.

"What kind of man does she take me to be? Have I been so mean that Jalesia could not have told me this? When am I supposed to find out about this? After we're married? If it's games Jalesia want to play, count me in. I need to know what she really thinks about me. If you tell her anything, I really mean it, you and Jalesia can move on out of my life."

Derrick reached for Zephanie's hand,

"Come on, I will walk you out. I need to check up on my deceiving fiancé. I can't believe this, I have sold out to this woman. I have committed the rest of my life to someone that I can't trust. Well, we will see where this circus leads me. I can't wait to see what Jalesia has up her sleeve."

After Zephanie left, Derrick walked into the bathroom where Jalesia was. He knocked on the door. Jalesia yelled through the door,

"You can come in, but I am not dressed yet."

When Derrick walked in Jalesia had on her bathrobe over her

bra and panties, and the bathrobe was slightly open. Jalesia spoke seductively,

"Let me close this bathrobe before we get in trouble."

Derrick replied in a cold harsh tone,

"You don't have anything to worry about. I am completely under control."

Derrick walked around Jalesia as he gave her a cold hard stare and said,

"So, how are you feeling now that the assailant has been locked away?"

Jalesia reached for Derrick and wrapped her arms around his neck. She firmly pressed her body against his body. She then opened her bathrobe and wrapped Derrick in the robe with her as she pulled his head down to give him a full mouth kiss.

Derrick's response was still cold.

Jalesia could sense that something was wrong, and she backed away and asked,

"Are you ok?"

"Yes, I am fine. What about you?"

Jalesia lifted her hands and spun around,

"Derrick, I feel so much better. The talk with Zephanie on yesterday, and finally putting the closure on the assailant has really helped me."

Jalesia walked up to Derrick and put her arms around his waist, and squeezed him tightly. She laid her head on his chest and said,

"Also, having my fine, handsome fiancé with me, makes life easier."

Derrick kept his hands in his pockets as his eyes became darker, and his face twisted with disgust. He pulled away and said,

"I sure am glad you are feeling better, but excuse me so I can go and get dressed."

Jalesia walked out of the bathroom, and into the bedroom, and started putting on her clothes. Derrick did not leave the room, even when Jalesia took off her robe and bared her body, with her matching light blue lace and silk panties and bra. Jalesia sat on the chaise and started putting on her panty hose. Derrick continued to stare with a look of disgust on his face. When Jalesia finally looked up to see his face, he was standing with his hands in his pockets still glaring at her. After Jalesia put her panty hose on, she walked over to Derrick and spoke softly,

"Sweetheart, are you ok? You look like you are sick. We don't have to go out tonight. We can stay in, if you're not feeling well."

Jalesia reached up to feel Derrick's forehead with the back of her hand, and he turned and walked away. When Derrick left the room, Jalesia picked up her robe and followed him.

Derrick walked into his bedroom, and stretched out across his bed. When Jalesia walked in she sat next to Derrick on the bed. She rubbed Derrick's head and spoke softly,

"Honey, what is wrong? I have never seen you like this before. Are you angry with me? Did I do something to upset you? What happened while I was taking my bath?"

Derrick did not answer. He did not respond to any of Jalesia's questions, as she continued to talk,

"Derrick, it is obvious I have done something that I don't know anything about. Sweetheart, please talk to me. I really don't know what I have done wrong. Did I say something in front of Zephanie that upset you? I can tell by the look you gave me in the bathroom that your are extremely upset with me."

Jalesia closed her eyes, and took a deep breath. She and Derrick sat in total silence until finally a knock on the door interrupted the silence. Jalesia got up to answer the door. It was Zephanie. Zephanie walked in smiling and said,

"I forgot my hair pins."

"Zephanie, those pins could have waited, or I could have brought them with me."

Zephanie replied,

"I hurried and got dress. I did not want to be sitting around waiting on Michael. And why aren't you dressed yet?"

Jalesia answered,

"I was talking with Derrick and I don't believe he is feeling well. I have never seen him this way before. I don't know what is wrong, because he's not talking to me."

Zephanie walked towards Derrick's room,

"You can go ahead and get dressed, and I will take a look at him.

Maybe I can prescribe something for him, if he's not feeling well."

Jalesia went into the room and began getting dressed, and Zephanie went into Derrick's room. Derrick was lying across the bed, and Zephanie closed the door behind her. Zephanie spoke in a whisper as she rubbed Derrick's leg,

"Derrick, would you please let me help you?"

Derrick turned over in the bed to face Zephanie and asked,

"What did she tell you about being raped? Did she enjoy it?"

Zephanie's mouth fell opened and she replied,

"Oh my God! Derrick, that is such a cruel thing to say. How can you be so cruel? No, she did not enjoy it, and I can't believe you would say something like that, even out of anger. She has been through a lot. This has not been an easy experience for her at all. I am really surprised tonight from that comment you made. This woman was a virgin, and then to have someone rob you of your virginity, that is very painful."

Derrick continued with his cold harsh attitude,

"If she did not enjoy it, or want more, why is she hiding? Why do I have to hear about this on the news? I should have been given a choice as to how to handle this situation."

After a long pause, Zephanie looked directly at Derrick and said,

"It's all about you, Derrick Curtis Dubois. I'm sorry, if I don't know anything else, but I do know Jalesia loves you. If she felt telling you before now would have been better for you, I know she would have told you. With the attitude you have right now, I don't know if any time would have been a good time for you."

Derrick was extremely angry as he spoke,

"Zephanie, what are you saying? Are you saying that Jalesia has to pick a time to tell me things, because I can't handle it?"

"No, Derrick, that is not what I am saying. You have to realize the one thing that Jalesia had always wanted to do, was to give her husband a virgin wife for his wedding gift, and that was taken away from her. Gone, because of one man's anger."

Derrick lifted his hand and intertwined his fingers behind his head, and spoke through clenched teeth,

"Listen to what I am saying. That woman is to be my wife, and she does not trust me enough to tell me everything. I am not angry because of what happened, I am angry because she deceived me."

Zephanie's voice shifted to more of a pleading voice,

"Derrick, she does trust you. Some things are about timing, and you don't understand the trauma involved with this situation. Please try to understand it has nothing to do with her trying to deceive you, because she had a ton of different emotions. Would it be easy for you to tell her if you had been raped?"

Derrick walked towards the door and quickly turned around,

"So why is it that you know, and I don't?"

Zephanie shrugged her shoulder and said,

"Derrick it's obvious I know, because I was her examining doctor. I was there from the time they rolled her into the hospital, up until now."

Derrick calmed down a little and said,

"Okay, I will give her the benefit of the doubt, and say it is all about timing, but if her mother knows and I don't know, then I will have a better understanding of where I stand. I will call her mother tonight, and then I will be clear on a lot of things."

Zephanie sucked her teeth, and starred at Derrick,

"That is so unfair. Michael and I have been married for almost five years, and there are some things my mom knows that Michael does not know."

Derrick was still pacing the floor with his hands in his pockets,

"Okay, if you were in a situation like this, would you tell Michael or would you tell your mother?"

Zephanie became angry,

"Now you wait just one minute. I have been in a situation like this, and Michael and I were married, and I went straight to my mom. She was the one to encourage me to tell Michael. No, I did not tell Michael immediately, because I did not know how he would react. A mother and daughter relationship can never be understood by a man. You will never be able to figure that out. A mother knows when her daughter is hurt, she knows what to say and how to say it. God has given something special to a mother and her daughter. Sons are important, but they have a different kind of bond."

Derrick looked down at his watch and looked back at Zephanie,

"Look, we have been in this room too long. I will do some evaluating on my own, and decide what I need to do. For now I will be on my best behavior, and go to the restaurant. I will be heading back to Tampa tonight, so I can think about this situation alone. I will call her mother tonight, because there are some things I need to know."

Derrick walked to the door and held the door open for Zephanie to exit. He went back into the room to get dressed.

All during dinner, Derrick had a glaring look at Jalesia. She would try to hold his hand but he would find a way to pull away. When she talked with Derrick, he was short and abrupt. Michael could sense the tension and he asked,

"Derrick, are you alright? This is a fine restaurant you have here. I wish I had the business sense to do something like this. I am an architect, and I design buildings like this for other people, and I need to put something like this together for me."

Derrick nodded his head in agreement,

"If you are the designer, then all you need are funds to start a project of your own. Maybe when you move to Florida, we can sit down and work up a plan in Tampa."

Michael responded with excitement,

"That sounds like an excellent ideal!"

During dinner, Derrick called the airlines to get a flight back to Tampa. He was placed on stand-by for first class. Jalesia thought they were going to spend the night in New York, and he was going to show her around the town. Jalesia asked,

"Derrick, did you want to leave so soon? I thought we were going to stay in New York a couple of days."

Derrick did not respond at first, but remembered what he said, that he would be on his best behavior.

"No Jalesia, I want to go home as soon as I possibly can. Please excuse me. I need to make a long distance phone call. I will be right back."

Michael could sense that Zephanie needed some time alone with Jalesia, so he excused himself also,

"Ladies, please excuse me, but I need to go to the men room, and walk around to admire this place."

After Michael left the table, that allowed Zephanie time to talk,

"Jalesia, did you tell your mother that your were raped?"

Jalesia answered,

"Yes, I finally broke down that Thursday night before you came to Tampa. I was over to Derrick's, and I could not sleep, so I called my mother that night to get it all off my chest."

Zephanie's expression showed disappointment,

"Darn it!"

"What is that all about?"

"I just hate that you have not told Derrick yet. When do you plan to tell him?"

Jalesia raised her eyebrow,

"Funny you would ask me that, because once things ended today, I decided I would tell him after we're married."

Derrick went into his office and called Rosa. Rosa answered the phone,

"Hello, this is the Brantz residence."

"Hi Mother, this is Derrick."

"Derrick, is everything alright? How did it go today?"

"It went fine. I'm calling, because I want to know if Jalesia told you the whole story?"

Rosa had a puzzled look on her face, and could sense something was going on,

"Yes Derrick, she told me the whole story. You were here with me when she told us. She told us how that cruel man punched and kicked her, and how he spit in her face. She talked about how the man put the gun in her mouth, and threaten to kill her. Derrick, we have gone over this before. Is my child alright?"

"Yes Mother, she is fine; in fact, we're at the restaurant now and we're trying to get a flight home tonight."

Rosa took a deep breath,

"I thought you were going to show Lea around New York. Don't be in a hurry to get back. Why don't you two just take some time and spend it together?"

Derrick answered,

"We have many years ahead to get to know one another better, but for now I want to be home. Mother, I need to be getting back to my guest. I will see you when we get home. Goodnight mother."

"Goodnight son."

Chapter Thirty-two

*D*errick and Jalesia arrived at their house in Tampa. Once inside the house, Jalesia got dressed for bed. She was sitting on the couch with her heels kicked up listening to gospel music. Derrick walked into the room and sat on the lounge chair across from her and said,

"Before you get sleepy, we need to talk."

Jalesia picked up the remote control and turned the volume down on the CD player. She motioned for Derrick to sit next to her on the sofa.

"Sweetheart, come and join me on the sofa. You have my undivided attention."

Derrick shook his head no and said,

"No, I'll stay right here, because what I need to say, I don't want to sit so close to you."

The smile slid off Jalesia's face,

"Wow! I guess this is a continuation from our trip in New York."

Derrick's voice was still harsh and cold,

"I think it will be better for us to remain away from each other until we are married. Then we can spend morning, noon and night together."

"Derrick something about what you said did not sound right. Are you angry at me about something? If so I don't know what it could be. It seems like you are being very cold with me."

Derrick answered,

"No, I am not being cold. I feel it's the best thing for us to do. Who knows, maybe you need time to evaluate our situation, and decide if I am truly the man you want to spend the rest of your life with. Maybe we did move too fast. Perhaps some time apart will give you an opportunity to think about us."

Jalesia spoke quickly as she got up and knelt down besides the lounge chair where Derrick was sitting. She rubbed Derrick's arm and spoke softly,

"Derrick, I don't need time apart from you. I don't have to evaluate our situation. My mind is certainly made up. I know I want to spend the rest of my life here on earth with you. Derrick Curtis Dubois, I need you in my life. What ever you want me to do, I will do it. I don't want to be away from you."

After a long pause, Jalesia looked directly into Derrick's eye and continued,

"I don't know what has happened, but I do love you. I don't want no other man, and never will. I feel like I have done something to you, but I don't know what it is. If I knew what I did wrong, while I am down here on bended knees I would beg you for forgiveness."

Jalesia put her arms around Derrick. He looked up at the ceiling and did not responded.

"Derrick, you haven't hugged nor kissed me yesterday and all day today. It's amazing you have barley talked to me."

Derrick closed his eyes and took a deep breath, and kissed Jalesia on the forehead as he stood up. His voice was blunt,

"I'm going to say goodnight."

Derrick walked out of the family room, and went into his bedroom and closed the door. Jalesia sat there still stunned at Derrick's reaction. She went into the master bedroom and said her prayers, and crawled into the bed.

Jalesia was laying in the bed for about an hour, but could not go to sleep. She thought to herself,

"It is amazing now that I have put the rapist behind me and I can finally sleep at night, and then this happens. My fiancé totally shuts me out of his life, and gives me the silent treatment."

Jalesia eased out of bed. She slid her feet in her bedroom shoes and walked over to Derrick's room. When she opened the door to Derrick's bedroom, he was sound asleep. Jalesia went back to her room. It was approximately two o'clock in the morning, when Jalesia called New York to speak with Zephanie. Michael answered the phone,

"Michael, I am sorry to wake you. This is Jalesia. May I please speak with Zephanie?"

"Sure you may. Is everything okay?"

"It will be alright."

Zephanie came on the phone,

"J, hold on a minute and let me go to another room."

When Zephanie came back to the phone, she spoke in a whisper. "Is everything ok?"

"No, Derrick asked me to allow him some time alone."

"What does he mean time alone?"

"He wants me away from him until we're closer to our wedding day."

Zephanie sat up straight and cleared her head,

"Help me understand. Is this because he feels pressured about making love to you when he is around you, or what?"

"No, it's not like that, in fact, I think he can't stand me right now. He is barley talking to me. I asked him about hugging and kissing me, but he ignored me. I love Derrick, but I am not crying about a lot of things anymore. The other day when I cried long and hard, I was able to release a lot of emotions. I refuse to make myself sick, by doing a lot of crying. I will continue to pray and leave these situations in God's hand. If God can't fix it, it can't be fixed.

Zephanie, I am sorry for disturbing you. I feel better after releasing that little bit off my chest. Thanks for listening to me once again. I am going to be all right. Keep me in your prayers."

"J, if you need me, please don't hesitate, just pick up the phone and call me. I am here for you."

Jalesia responded,

"I know you are here for me. I am going to say good night, so you can get your rest."

"Good night."

Chapter Thirty-three

Sunday morning had finally arrived. Jalesia had a restless night thinking about Derrick. She got up to start her day. Derrick was already up and dressed for church. He was sitting in the kitchen eating breakfast and looking through the Sunday morning paper.

Jalesia walked into the kitchen with her hair still wrapped in her silk scarf and her robe over her nightgown. She walked over to Derrick and took the newspaper out of his hand. She moved his plate to the other side of the table, and sat in his lap. Jalesia look Derrick in his eyes and said,

"Good morning, my soon to be husband. I am not going to let go that easily. Whatever you are mad at me about, we need to discuss it. I have prayed and ask God to help us with our situation."

Jalesia paused and put both of her hands on Derrick's cheeks and lightly kissed him on the lips. She did not feel Derrick respond; therefore, she tried to lightly kiss him on the lips again, but again no response. She then leaned forward and rested her lips on Derrick's lips to see if he would kiss her back, but he did not.

A lump grew in Jalesia's throat as she spoke with tears in the well of her eyes,

"Derrick, this is unbelievable. I would have never known that you could be so hard and cold to me. You have totally shut me out. I am pleading with you to tell me what have I done to you, to make you treat me this way."

Derrick shrugged his shoulder, but did not respond. Jalesia asked as the tears rolled down her cheeks,

"All I want to know is do you still love me? All the other things do not matter at this point. Last night you asked me to leave and I will honor your request to give you the time that you need. Derrick, I really need to know, do you still love me?"

Jalesia stood up and put both her hands on her head as the tears continued to fall,

"Derrick, please stop treating me this way. I love you with all of my heart, and I really need you right now. DO YOU STILL LOVE ME?"

Derrick closed his eyes as he fought back his tears, but did not say a word. Jalesia put her face in her hands and began to cry,

"Derrick, I would have never known I could have done anything to you, to make you stop loving me. I thought you loved me as much as I love you. I don't know what it could be because you will not tell me. But if you want me to leave, I will respect your request.

Don't worry about taking me home. I will get there, but I want you to know I still love you, and I always will. I can't do anything about why you are upset with me, because I don't know why. On tomorrow, I will stop our wedding plans. For us to be Christians, it is unbelievable for us to allow the enemy to come into our lives and disrupt our communication."

Derrick finally spoke with anger,

"So you don't want to marry me, huh?"

"Derrick, I do want to marry you. I can't think of anything more that I want to do, but I can't marry you if you don't love me."

Derrick continued in anger,

"Did I one time tell you that I don't love you? But if you want to call off the wedding, go right ahead!"

Jalesia was still pleading with Derrick,

"Sweetheart, why are you so upset with me? I don't want to call off the wedding. I thought that was something you wanted."

Derrick looked down at his watch and said,

"I need to be going to church. We can talk about this later. I do not want to discuss this any more."

Jalesia followed Derrick to the door, and she could feel that

Derrick really did not want her to leave.

"Honey, when you return I will be gone. I will give you that time away from me that you need."

Derrick was still angry as he further added,

"If you leave, don't call your mother to pick you up. Just take one of our vehicles and keep it until you come back."

Derrick turned to walk out the door, and Jalesia called him soft and sincerely,

"Derrick,"

She paused and took a deep breath.

"If you love me, would you tell me that you love me?"

Derrick stopped and turned around. He grabbed his keys and walked out the door. He got in his car and drove off. Jalesia closed the door behind her and walked into the bedroom to get her things. She wiped her tears, and took a deep breath as she pulled herself together.

When Jalesia got her things together, she decided she would drive the Lincoln. Once Inside of the Lincoln, Derrick left a note saying, "I do love you." Jalesia balled up the note and threw it to the passenger seat.

Derrick had made Jalesia a CD that she listened to as she drove home.

This Sunday was Women's Day, and the women were in charge. When Evangelist Hargrett got up to bring the message, she looked directly at Jalesia. When she gave her theme for the morning she pointed to Jalesia. "Keep the Joy." She began to say, "Our inward attitude does not reflect our outward circumstance. Joy is the result of peace with God. Happiness and Joy are two different emotions. Happiness depends on happenings or circumstance, but joy depends on Christ." She closed her Bible and continued, "Happiness is walking hand and hand with the one that you love, or opening a gift on Christmas morning, or vacationing on your favorite island, or getting that diamond ring you always desired, or having a birthday party and everyone is shouting Happy Birthday to you. We chase after happiness by spending a lot of money, or searching for new experiences. What happens when love ones walk out and leave you, or the gift breaks, or the diamond ring is lost, or the money is gone, or they turn off the lights, and the party's over. Often time happiness gets up and leave. But in contrast to happiness stands JOY. Joy is confident assurance of God's love, and work in our lives. Knowing that He will be there no matter what. No matter how things look, Jesus will be there. Happiness depends on happenings, but joy depends on Jesus Christ.

"Keep the Joy!"

When Evangelist Hargrett sat down, the choir began to sing, *'This joy that I have the world didn't give it to me, the world didn't give it and the world can't take it away.'*

The church erupted with praises. People were clapping and shouting, and praising God in their own way. Jalesia stood to her feet and raised her hands in the air, and the tears ran down her cheeks.

The drive home was great. Jalesia was praising God all the way home. Once she arrived home she changed into more comfortable clothing, and met Rosa in the kitchen. They talked about the wedding plans. Jalesia did not tell Rosa what she and Derrick were going through.

After Rosa was done preparing dinner, Jalesia went into her bedroom to call Derrick. Derrick's answering machine picked up, and Jalesia left a message,

"Hi sweetheart. It's me. When you get a chance, please give me a call. Also, have I told you lately that I love you? Church was really good today. I wish you could have been there. I really need to talk to you about something very important. You may not want to be with me any more, but I think you should know. I love you. Will you please call me?"

Chapter Thirty-four

Three days had passed and Derrick still had not called Jalesia. Jalesia continued with the wedding plans as she and Derrick had discussed. Jalesia called Dianiece, her sister and wedding coordinator, to discuss how she wanted the reception to be done.

Jalesia tried calling Derrick again, and there was still no answer. She left another message,

"Hello sweetheart, I needed to discuss with you times and dates for the fitting of your tuxedo. The tuxedo company called, and they are going to need enough time to prepare all the tuxedos for the ushers and the best man. They need all of you to come in for your fitting.

Derrick, this is really getting hard for me, because you will not communicate with me. I miss you, and I love you. I wish you would tell me that you love me, and life will be so much easier. Call me once you get a chance. I love you. Bye, Sweetheart."

There was a knock at the door. Jalesia raced to the door hoping it was Derrick. When she answered the door, it was Zephanie. They greeted one another with a hug. Jalesia was so excited to see Zephanie, and Jalesia asked,

"What storm blew you down here?"

Zephanie responded,

"Desperate time calls for desperate measures. I need you to get some clothes to spend about three days with me."

After their conversation, Jalesia went into the room to gather her things. Rosa walked into the living room, and she and Zephanie warmly embraced one another. Rosa said,

"Hello Zephanie. What are you doing in town?"

"Mother, I am here taking care of some business. I am going to be transferred to one of the hospitals here in Tampa. Also, I am going to hang out with Jalesia for a few days. Mother, it is very, very, very important, if you see or hear from Derrick, do not let him know that I am here."

Rosa responded,

"I can follow directions, but what is going on?"

"I need to talk with Jalesia about Derrick and the wedding."

By this time Jalesia was walking back into the room, as Zephanie continued,

"Mother, we will talk later. Everything is okay. I just wanted to spend some time with my girl. I have a few days off, and I need some rest and relaxation."

Zephanie had a suite on Clearwater beach. When they got to the suite, She and Jalesia sat out on the balcony that over looked the crowded beach, as they each sip on their virgin pina coladas. It was spring break, and the beach was packed with college students.

Jalesia smiled at Zephanie and then asked,

"Zephanie, what really brought you this way?"

Zephanie moved her chair closer to Jalesia, and put her hand on top of Jalesia's hand and said,

"What really brought me here was the hospital paying for this suite. They were trying to impress me so that I would accept their proposal. And since I am here, I thought it would be an excellent time for you and I to talk. When you and Derrick were in New York, and while you were taking your bath, Derrick heard the story on the news about you being rape.

I told you some time ago to tell Derrick the whole story about you being raped, because you would not want him to hear it from someone else. Derrick and I talked about it, and he told me he wanted to see how long you were going to deceive him. I defended you, but Derrick did not want to hear it. I prayed about this whole situation, and I would be less than a sister not to tell you. I told

Michael and your mother if they hear from Derrick, not to tell him I am here.

Derrick threatened me, and said if I revealed to you that he knew you were deceiving him he would not want to marry you.

That brings me to today. I feel that you are my sister, and I don't care what Derrick said. I think you should know, and here I am. I feel so bad, because as I thought about it, I feel I should have told you from the start, but I really did not want you and Derrick's relationship to end over something so petty. I understand Derrick's hurt, but I feel that the two of you should have been able to talk and pray through this situation."

Jalesia stood up and lifted her hands to the Lord and said,

"Thank you Lord! Now I understand."

Jalesia sat back down, then turned to Zephanie,

"Zep, thanks for being led by the Lord. When I was in church on Sunday, the Lord told me to tell Derrick the whole story and not wait until we are married. The Lord let me know that out of all fairness, Derrick should have the choice if he wants to be with me or not. I made up in my mind I would tell him, even if I loose him. I have made several attempts to contact Derrick, but he will not return any of my calls."

Zephanie held Jalesia's hand and softly spoke,

"As long as the Lord knows you have done what He told you to do, that's all that matters. Just remain patient, God will deal with Mr. Dubois."

Zephanie and Jalesia spent three days together hanging out and talking about men. They discussed how you have to handle men.

Zephanie explained,

"You have to be submissive to men in a way where you are the one who is really in control. They don't know you are in control, but you know you are in control."

Chapter Thirty-five

*W*hile in church this Sunday, Derrick was singing along with the choir. He began to think to himself,

"Wow! I must have really been mean these past few days. I really do love Jalesia, but I can't believe that she would deceive me. I have poured out my heart to her, and she can keep this from me? Maybe Zephanie is right. Maybe Jalesia is trying to find the right time. Zephanie brought out a good point when she asked me if I had been raped, would I have been eager to tell anyone.

The message today from Pastor Johns was intended for me. The Lord was talking directly to me. Pastor Johns was saying how the Lord love us so much, while we were yet sinners, Christ died for us. No greater love have no man than that he would lay down his life for his friends. His theme was, "Love Is What It Does."

Pastor Johns was telling us that God so loved the world that He gave His only begotten Son. Love is not always what I can get, but what I can give. We must forgive if we want to be forgiven. And how sometimes, but by the grace of God it could be some of us that could be in a situation that could cause great embarrassment, or great shame. But God saw fit not to allow us to go through some of those trying times, and the least we can do is show someone else the love that we would want in a trying situation."

Derrick continued to think to himself as he shifted in his seat,

"I hope Jalesia continue with the wedding plans while I am

away. I will be leaving going on my businessman conference, and when I return to Florida it will be a few days before the wedding. I hope I have not upset Jalesia enough to make her stop loving me. I really am sorry, and I really need to call her and let her know that I apologize for being a butt these past few days. I felt so bad when I walked out on her, and I did not tell her that I love her, but I will make it up to her. Jalesia has been through a lot, and I should have been there for her when she needed me the most. I could kick my own selfish butt."

Derrick hit his forehead with the palm of his hand,

"How could I be so cold to someone that loves me so much?"

Derrick could not get Jalesia off his mind. He thought of all the happy times they had shared together. He thought that he was selfish, and he should have been able to understand that Jalesia had a reason why she did not tell him what she was going through.

"How will I ever be able to make this up to Jalesia?"

Derrick further thought to himself,

"If it had been me, I'm sure she would have been there for me, every step of the way."

Derrick returned home and packed his suitcase for his business trip. He stretched out on the couch to get a quick nap before his flight was scheduled to leave.

Derrick's phone rang and he answered in his sexy, husky voice,

"Hello sweetheart."

Jalesia was stunned that Derrick called her sweetheart. She lifted her hands to the Lord and said a silent 'Thank you Jesus!'

"Hi honey. How are you?"

Derrick responded with a smile in his voice,

"I'm doing fine. Have you missed me?"

Jalesia got really excited,

"Yes, of course I miss you! If you let me come over, I will show you just how much I miss you. Can I come over? I really need to talk with you."

Derrick sat up on the sofa,

"No sweetheart. Now is not a good time."

Jalesia was overly excited, while trying to sound calm on the phone,

"Honey, were you busy?"

Derrick answered,

"Yes and No. I was trying to get me a nap in. I need to talk with you also."

"Oh Derrick! I hope it's all good, because I can't take any more bad news from you."

Derrick continued to speak,

"I was in Church on yesterday, and I got spanked by the word of God, so I need to fix some things that I messed up."

Jalesia folded her hands together and began to plead,

"Derrick, can I please come over so we can talk?"

"Jalesia now is not a good time. I am extremely sleepy. We will get together some other time. I will be leaving in a few minutes going out of town."

"No Derrick, you can't. We need to get together and make up with a few hugs and kisses before you leave."

Derrick sat up on the sofa and said,

"Please forgive me for the way I have acted lately. Pastor Johns was speaking directly to me today. I realize my actions were not pleasing to God. I promise you when I return in about six week, we will make up with plenty of hugs and kisses."

Jalesia responded with a surprised tone,

"Six weeks? Where are you going?"

"These are the only trips that are mandatory every year for business men. I have seminars to attend. I will be in Texas for four weeks, and then in Louisiana for two weeks."

Jalesia was disappointed,

"Derrick, that is too close to our wedding day. Can I go with you?"

Derrick's voice was apologetic,

"My flight is already booked, and I will be leaving shortly heading to the airport."

Jalesia asked surprisingly,

"Today? When were you going to tell me you were leaving for your trip?"

Derrick answered,

"When I was upset with you, I was not going to tell you at all. I was going to let you know once I got there."

Jalesia was still pleading,

"Derrick, I need to see you before you go. You can't just leave me for six weeks, and I don't have the opportunity to get a hug and a kiss. I have not heard you tell me that you love me."

Derrick answered,

"Jalesia, I do love you. But there is no way for you to get a hug and a kiss because we don't have enough time to meet."

Jalesia held up her finger with a bright idea,

"Derrick, I have a good idea. Please, let me meet you in Texas."

Derrick shook his head no,

"Sweetheart that is not a good idea. It will get too *hot* in Texas if you are there. The best thing for the both of us would be for you not to be around me. If you were there, I would want to make love to you. So the best thing for the both of us would be to remain apart.

The Lord had helped me to get myself under control where I was not thinking about making love to you. I had it together. I knew I would be able to hold out until we are married. But because of my disobedience, I am all bothered in my body again. So your answer about meeting me in Texas is No, No, and No! I will be fasting and praying, and going before the Lord to get myself under control again. Jalesia, I do love you. I remembered something Pastor Hamilton said about not allowing anything to hinder our communication."

Jalesia started crying as her voice trembled,

"I promise if I come over I will not stay long. You can schedule a later flight, so we can get together and talk. I really need a hug from you Derrick. Just one hug and I won't even kiss you. I just want to be held in your arms. Please Derrick, I could have been there by now."

Derrick stood up and walked into the bedroom,

"I know you could have been here by now Jalesia, but I am running late. I promise I will see you as soon as I get back home. Nothing could stop me from seeing you as soon as I get back, but in the meantime I will call you everyday. Would you come back home to our house? I will not be here, but I want you here."

Jalesia continued to smile,

"Sure I'll come back home. Sweetheart, tell me that you love me again."

Derrick responded,

"Miss Jalesia Anna Brantz, soon to be Mrs. Jalesia Anna Dubois, I, Derrick Curtis Dubois, love you with all my heart. I look forward to the day when you will be my wife. Look, I got to go. I promise I will talk with you later. I love you. Bye Sweetie."

"Bye sweetheart."

Chapter Thirty-six

*J*alesia had been extremely busy for the last month. She had been running around with Dianiece getting everything situated for the wedding and the reception. Zephanie and Michael had bought an inventory home in a sub-division approximately ten minutes from Derrick's community. They were planning to move in this weekend. Derrick was preparing to leave Texas going to Louisiana to complete his business owner's conference. Derrick and Jalesia talked every night. Derrick missed his tuxedo fitting. The other guys in the wedding party had been fitted for their tuxedos. Jalesia had been spending time at Derrick's house. Now that the wedding was a month away, she thought it would be best for her to leave once Derrick returned home. She did not want to tempt Derrick. Neither did she want to be tempted.

Derrick was on the phone with his mother, Shirley. Shirley had always been concerned with the women Derrick dated. She had always been overly protective about Derrick's money.

Shirley was sitting at the dining room table while she talked with Derrick on the phone,

"Derrick, have you done a thorough back ground search on this young lady? I know you said she is not interested in your money. Are you sure this is the woman for you? I don't think she loves you like you love her."

Derrick was a little upset with Shirley for challenging his decision.

"Mom, everything is going as planned. I love Jalesia and she loves me. She does not love me for the money. It's amazing to me that you think it's always about the money. I am going to marry her."

Shirley began to talk to Derrick in a softer tone. She could sense that Derrick was getting a little on the defense.

"Derrick, I'm not saying Jalesia is like that but a lot of women will not marry for love, but for money."

Derrick answered,

"Mom, I know Jalesia loves me. I am just sorry that I put her through so much because of what you thought. I almost lost Jalesia because I let you dictate to me on how I should test her love. You told me to make her prove to me that she loves me. I should have never played that game. I should have followed my first mind and went to Jalesia and asked her what I wanted to know. I am sure she would have told me the truth. I already know that Jalesia loves me. If I find out later that she was in this relationship for the money, then that's my bad. From this day forward, I will be completely honest with her and I know she will be completely honest with me. I will not be the one to hurt her again. I don't like playing games. Having the Lord on the inside, you can discern if a person loves you or not."

Shirley became apologetic,

"Derrick, you are right. No one wants to be challenged on the love they have for another person. I did not want to see my child hurt. I can see how much you love Jalesia. I never intended for you to play games. When you came to me and told me how Jalesia had hurt you, I wanted her to prove her love before you got any deeper. Baby, I'm sorry. I realize how much you love Jalesia. Any woman you love, I love her also." Shirley started laughing and said,

"Your nose is so far open you can just about drive a truck through it. I believe Jalesia love you, just as much as you love her."

Derrick started smiling and said,

"I'm cute, I'm fine, I'm packing junk in my trunk. I have a little money. Need I say more? Jalesia is not going anywhere. For what reason would she need to look anywhere else? She has everything she need, or could ever want in a man. And it's found right here in me."

Shirley began smiling,

"You are just like your dad. He always said silly things like that.

If you feel Jalesia loves you, then that is your reason for marriage. I am here for you no matter what. I am going to pay Miss Thang a visit so I can see how she really is. After I see about Ms. Jalesia, you are on your own. I just want her to know that I love my son and I am not going to stand by and let any one hurt him."

Derrick wanted to get off the phone so he would have time to speak with Jalesia before he got sleepy.

"Mom, I would love for you to speak with Jalesia. She needs to know how nosey you are now, so she will not have any surprises once we are married. I know that Jalesia is so down to earth that you will love her. Mom, I would love to talk longer but I am getting sleepy, and I need to call Jalesia before I go to sleep."

"O.K. Derrick. Be safe and I will see you when you return. Good-bye."

As soon as Derrick hung up the phone with his mother, he called Jalesia. She answered the phone as if she was expecting his call,

"Hello, my soon to be husband."

Derrick responded in a tired voice,

"Hi hon. Yes, it's me. I am extremely tired. I just got off the phone talking about you. I was telling someone how you put up with my crap and how much you love me."

Jalesia answered as if she was ready for a long conversation,

"You told them the truth about me loving you, but you don't make me go through a lot of crap. We had just one minor difficulty, but thanks be to God it's over now. And by the way, to whom were you talking to?"

Derrick responded like a schoolboy that had a secret.

"I am not telling. You will know for yourself soon enough."

Jalesia shifted to a more meaningful conversation,

"Is the conference now over in Texas?"

Derrick answered,

"Yes, we finished up today. In the morning I will be heading to Louisiana. I am so bored. I still have another conference to attend. Next year will be better because you will be there with me."

Jalesia began to feel her tiredness,

"I am a little tired also, but my tiredness is not from boredom. I have been extremely busy helping Dianiece get everything ready for our wedding day."

Derrick was undressing while he was talking on the phone. He fell across the bed with just his tee shirt and underwear. He continued to talk,

"Sweetheart, I have gotten in my relax position and I don't want to fall asleep on you, so I better say good night because I am really tired."

Jalesia snapped her finger and her eyebrows curled up,

"Derrick, one more thing before we hang up. What are we going to do about your tuxedo? You missed your fitting."

Derrick was so sleepy he could barley keep his eyes open as he responded,

"Sweetheart, I have already bought my tuxedo here in Texas. You don't have to worry about me. I am not a forgetful person. I have already taken care of myself."

Derrick started talking out of his head and breathing heavy. Jalesia tried calling him a couple of times but he did not respond. Derrick had drifted off to sleep. She could not get mad because he had warned her that he was sleepy and needed to go. Jalesia gently placed the receiver in its cradle and turned over to go to sleep. She began thinking about how much she loves Derrick.

Chapter Thirty-seven

*T*he doorbell rang and startled Jalesia out of her sleep. Jalesia grabbed her robe and dashed to the front door. She glanced out of the peephole, and saw that it was Derrick's mom, Shirley, who was standing at the door holding a basket. Jalesia shouted through the door,

"Mrs. Shirley, hold on for just a moment. I need to disarm the security system."

Jalesia disarmed the system and opened the door,

"Good morning Mrs. Shirley. Come on in."

Shirley walked in and kissed Jalesia on the cheek. She greeted her with a cheerful tone.

"Good morning sweetie pie. I came over today so we can talk. I had to do this now, because I don't plan to make visits once you and Derrick are married. I don't want to walk up on something like you two trying to produce me a grandchild."

Shirley winked at Jalesia and laughed at her own joke.

Jalesia forced a smile and helped Shirley with the basket. She walked into the kitchen and put the basket on the table. Jalesia could tell this was not going to be a short visit and she said,

"Mrs. Shirley, do you mind if I freshen up and come back to have this conversation with you? I have not brushed my teeth and wash my face yet. I don't want to offend you with morning breath."

Shirley answered,

"You go right ahead and I will be here when you get back. You're a cute girl even just waking up."

"Thank you. I will be right back."

While Jalesia was getting dressed, she was wondering,

"Why is Derrick's mom here, and why so early? This must be the early morning family, because Derrick wakes up in the morning playing and alert. Could Derrick have told his mom that we had a big fight? Did she want to give me some pointers on how to treat her son? Forget it. It is too early in the morning for trying to figure things out. The only way to find out what Mrs. Shirley wants is for me to go out there and see."

After Jalesia finished getting dressed, she walked into the kitchen. Shirley was sitting at the table eating a cinnamon crunch bagel. Jalesia had her hair down and wore a pair of jeans with an over sized buttoned down shirt. She talked in her most professional voice,

"So Mrs. Shirley, what do I owe for you to grace me with your pleasant smile this morning?"

Shirley answered as she continued to eat,

"I just stopped by to have a momma to daughter talk with you. I want to tell you first of all, if you so desire, you can call me momma. I just think Mrs. Shirley is too formal, especially when you are talking about family."

Shirley reached across the table and held Jalesia's hand,

"There are so many stereo type about black people, but with me, I know my family is a very loving and affectionate family. We don't mind kissing and hugging one another. I want to have another daughter, and not a daughter-in-law. I want us to have a very good relationship. I don't want you to feel when you see me coming, 'Oh no! Here comes Derrick's momma.' I want you to hang out with me, go to the mall, or we go places together. You can come over to my house anytime you want. You can call me whenever you need to. Derrick has always been really special to me. I love my son, and I want what is best for the both of you. I have never seen Derrick in love before, and when he talks to me, he is almost in tears describing the love he has for you. He was afraid because he did not think you loved him the same."

Shirley took a pause and Jalesia could finally speak. Jalesia shifted in her seat and took a deep sigh as she reached into the basket and put one of the bagels on her plate,

"Momma, thanks for coming over and being so honest with me. I do look forward to the times we will share with one another. I am relieved in one sense, because I did not know what was the nature of your visit. It is really nice to have your new momma come over and welcome you into the family. I look forward to the day when I become Mrs. Dubois. The love I have for Derrick is nothing I have ever experienced. He and I have discussed how scary it feels to love like we love. We have concluded that only God can put two people together, and they experience the love that we have. I love your son, and you never have to worry about me trying to hurt him intentionally. I think what you have done today is very nice."

Shirley looked at Jalesia and smiled,

"Girl, you talk more than I do. The two of you are equally in love. You're so in love the two of you could eat one another. Now don't take that literally."

Jalesia's face was flushed with embarrassment as Shirley continued,

"I have to admit to you, when I spoke to my son on last night, and he was telling me how much he loves you, I was a little concern that he was heading for a heartbreak. But after having talked with you today, I know now that Derrick was definitely right."

Shirley paused and continued as she began to laugh,

"When you talk with Derrick, ask him what did he mean when he said you loved him because he is cute, fine, packing junk in his trunk, and there is no one out there better for you."

Jalesia responded,

"I know he is cute, fine, and that there is no one else out there for me. But the packing junk in the trunk, I will not know about that until we're married."

Jalesia and Shirley sat around talking and getting to know one another better. Shirley had a lot of old childhood stories to tell Jalesia about Derrick. While they were talking, the phone rang and interrupted their conversation. Jalesia answered,

"Hello."

"Hey Honey. Have I told you lately that I love you?"

"Yes you have, but I wish you were here in person to tell me. You know you fell asleep on me last night? Our mom is here. We have been talking all morning. She has been telling me some of your childhood stories."

Derrick commented,

"Tell my momma I said to leave me alone. I thought it was something why my ears were burning. I just wanted you to know that I made it to Louisiana. I don't like it here, so as soon as I can, I will be leaving this place. I am so ready to get home to wrap my sweetie in my arms. I am under control once again. I will be able to hold out until we are married. Four more weeks and you will be mine. I will be here between two to three weeks. Then, when I get home I will prepare for the grandest day of my life. Jalesia, I love you. I really do feel sorry for my baby today, because if you had to sit and listen to my momma today, I feel for you. Momma can go a mile a minute."

"Derrick, I have really enjoyed you momma, and I have enjoyed the conversations we have had. Oh! Let me ask you, what did you mean when you said I am marrying you because you are cute, fine, and you're packing junk in the trunk?"

Derrick became embarrassed and asked to speak with his momma,

"Please put my momma on the phone."

Jalesia handed the phone to Shirley,

"He wants to speak with you."

Shirley answered,

"What do you want? Yes I said it!"

Derrick put on his humbled voice,

"Momma, you're not supposed to tell Jalesia everything. There are some things that we discuss, but I don't want Jalesia to know."

"Ok, I will tell her that too."

Derrick started begging,

"Momma, please don't! You are going to make me stop telling you things, because you talk too much. Momma, on a serious note, I am your son, and I know you don't want to spoil my marriage before I get married."

Shirley responded,

"You are right son. I know what to do, and what not to do. Remember I am your mother, and a mother knows all. You were right. I have really enjoyed myself talking to Jalesia. She is down to earth just like you said. I look forward to getting together with her and going shopping or just hanging out."

Derrick responded,

Momma would you please put Jalesia on the phone? You have me talking as much as you."

Shirley replied,

"Son, it is too late. You already talk as much as I do. Here is Jalesia."

Shirley handed the phone to Jalesia.

When Jalesia came back on the phone, Derrick continued to talk,

"Sweetheart, I am sorry. I really called to talk with you but I will call you later tonight. I will let you complete your conversation with momma. I Love you, I love you, I love you, and I am sorry you have to be tortured hearing all of my momma's boring stories."

"I love you too sweetheart. I really do miss you."

Derrick further added,

"Well, it's not as long as it was and it's not as short as I want it to be, but I will be coming home soon. Hey, get back to momma and I will call you later. Love you."

"Love you too, bye-bye."

Chapter Thirty-eight

*D*errick had finished seminar two days early. It was Wednesday night and Derrick could not wait to get to his suite. He wanted to call Jalesia so he could tell her that he would be coming home early.

Derrick called his house but Jalesia was not there. He then called Otis and Rosa's house. Rosa answered the phone,

"Good evening this is the Brantz residence, how may I help you?"

"Hi mother, this is Derrick. Is Jalesia at home?"

"No, she is still at your house. She may not be home, because she called me and told me she was going to the mall. She went to pick up a surprise for you. She should be back in about an hour. Is everything alright?"

" Yes mother, everything is alright. Our seminar is over, and I will be leaving in the morning on flight #1272. I am so excited about leaving. I wanted to share the good news with Jalesia. I'm on stand by for first class, but they have some available seats in coach. Just in case I don't talk to Jalesia, will you let her know for me?"

Rosa lifted her hand to her mouth with excitement. She knew Jalesia was going to be surprised, because the only thing she had been talking about is how happy she will be when Derrick gets home. Rosa grabbed a pen and piece of paper and wrote down the flight time and flight number.

"Derrick, she is going to be so happy to hear from you. Maybe you should try calling her back. This news is great news. She was not expecting you until late tomorrow night."

Derrick answered,

"I do plan to call her back. But I know once I get comfortable, I may fall asleep. I have my clock set for three-thirty so I can get up. I have to arrive at the airport early in order to check in for that six a.m. flight."

After Derrick hung up the phone with Rosa, he tried calling his house once again. Jalesia answered the phone,

"Hello."

"Hey sweetheart. I have some good news for you. The seminar is over and I will be leaving in the morning coming home. I am on stand-by for first class on the six a.m. flight to Tampa Florida. I am coming in on flight #1272. I can't wait to get home. Have on your kissing lips, because I am missing you something terribly. I will never again get angry with you like I did. We have so much we need to talk about. From now on I want you to be honest with me, and I will never shut you out again. I am going to wrap you in my arms and tell you one hundred times how much I love you."

Jalesia was sitting on the sofa with her legs folded underneath her butt and she responded,

"I am so excited! I just want you here with me. I bought you something today, and I just know you are going to love it."

Jalesia shifted to a more serious conversation, as she sat up on the sofa,

"Sweetheart, I realize you have money, and often times you want to buy the things you want. Sometimes the Lord will tell you no, but you don't want no for an answer, so you continue to pursue. Stop doing that. Trust God in every area of your life. The Lord always knows what's best for us, and we just have to accept His will. If you don't like God's answer, pray about it and see what He allows. I would rather be in God's perfect will than to be in His permissive will."

Derrick had a concerned look on his face. He knew what Jalesia said was true. He could not respond, because she was right. He has always thought that money could buy him everything. Derrick knew that spiritually Jalesia has it together, and that is another reason why he loves her so much.

Changing to yet another conversation, Jalesia continued,

"I enjoyed the conversation with your mother. She is a lot of fun. I see great days ahead for us. She talked to me about your sister and brother. She also told me about your father. We talked about so much I think I know more about the family than you do. Our conversation was interesting and she did not bore me at all."

Derrick took a deep sigh and said,

"Well my love, this time tomorrow we will be back together. I want to hear everything you and momma talked about. I don't want to discuss past problems. I want to leave what is in the past behind. What we did not do before now, we can't go back and fix it. From here on we move forward. I love you so much. I will be home tomorrow, and in a few days we will be married. I love you so much that just talking about it sends shivers down my spine. Since I have to be at the airport so early in the morning, I need to get some rest. I am going to say good night, and I love you."

Jalesia responded,

"Have you noticed that you always control the conversation? You are always the one to set the pace on when is a good time to hang up. Well Mr. Dubois, it is not happening that way tonight. I have a few things I would like to say."

Derrick extended his hand as if to say you have the floor,

"You are right. Thank you for bringing that to my attention. By habit I do find myself doing that. I am going to sit here and listen until you say good night."

Jalesia called Derrick's name soft and sincerely,

"Derrick?"

Derrick responded just as sincerely,

"Yes sweetheart. I am still here."

"Derrick, I love you. I want to be everything you want me to be as your wife. I really look forward to seeing you tomorrow. I want our lives together to be totally controlled by God."

Derrick responded,

"Sweetheart, thanks for the information you gave me earlier. I have to admit, you are exactly right. Often times I feel I am in control, but really I'm not. God truly is the one who is in control of my life, and from this day forward, I will seek Him the more in every situation."

Jalesia concluded,

"Now on that note, the remainder of this conversation will be completed when I am in your arms. I love you and I am going to say good night my love. "

"Good-night Sweetheart."

Chapter Thirty-nine

*I*t was now Thursday morning. Jalesia was in the bed sound asleep when she was suddenly awakened by a frantic knock at the front door. Then, some one began ringing the doorbell repeatedly, and calling Jalesia's name. Jalesia sat up in bed and tried to clear her head. The knocking became more intense, causing Jalesia to jump out of bed. She dashed over to the security control box and disarmed the house. She then ran to the front door. She shouted through the door,

"Who is it?"

Zephanie responded with a voice that was full of fright,

"J, open the door. It's me and mother."

Jalesia's heart began to race. She felt weak in her knees and her stomach began to churn. She reached for the knob to open the door. Rosa and Zephanie rushed into the house. Zephanie had her medical bag in her hand. Rosa then put her arms around Jalesia and pulled her into the family room. Jalesia could barely walk. She began screaming as the tears started flowing from her eyes,

"WHAT IS GOING ON? I know something is wrong because both of you are here looking like you have been crying. Somebody please tell me what is going on?"

Zephanie asked Jalesia,

"Have you seen the news this morning?"

Jalesia began to shake as she lifted her hands up to her face and screamed,

"OH MY GOD! Please don't give me any bad news. What happened? Somebody tell me what has happened."

The phone rang and Rosa answered,

"Hello?"

Jalesia listened to her mother's one side conversation. Jalesia eyes were stretched wide with fear as Rosa continued to talk,

"No, we have not told her but as soon as I get off the phone with you, we will tell her.

You can come over, but by the time you get here she will know."

After Rosa hung up the phone, Jalesia asked,

"Who was that?"

Rosa answered as she sat on the couch next to Jalesia,

"That was Shirley. This morning flight #1272 crashed, and there are no survivors."

Jalesia let out a loud scream, as she grabbed her heart,

"NOOOOOOO! OH MY GOD! HELP ME LORD!"

Jalesia began panting and gasping for air as she fell back on the sofa. Her body went limp as she fainted. Rosa held Jalesia's head up and Zephanie came over to attend to her medically.

Zephanie spoke softly to Rosa,

"She is okay. Not enough oxygen flowing through your blood and into your brain will cause you to faint. Let's lay her flat and raise her legs."

Zephanie looked at her watch and within two minutes Jalesia regained consciousness and said,

"PLEASE, PLEASE MOMMA, TELL ME THIS IS NOT TRUE. MOMMAAAAAA! MOMMAAAAAAA!"

Rosa laid Jalesia's head on her shoulder. She allowed her to cry as much as she needed as Rosa rocked her back and forth. Rosa brushed Jalesia's hair with her hand. Jalesia extended her arms toward Zephanie. She shouted across the room to Zephanie as the tears continued to fall,

"ZEPHANIE! Can you please tell me that this is not true? Please don't tell me that Derrick is dead. This can't be. I talked with him last night and he promised me that he would come home to be with me. Oh God! Please make this a bad dream. Oh God! Please don't do this to me. Lord, I can't take this. Please God, help me!"

Jalesia looked up towards heaven with her arms stretched,

"Oh God! Please, in the name of Jesus, don't let this be true. God, if I ever needed you, I need you now. I can't take another bad experience in my life. Wherever Derrick is, I want to be, so take me too."

Jalesia was still crying out of control when the knock came on the door. She stood up and ran towards the door, crying and shouting with her arm extended out,

"DERRICKKKK? God, please let that be Derrick."

Zephanie immediately caught Jalesia and wrapped her arms around her. She began to cry along with Jalesia,

"J, it's not Derrick. It's his mother. Babe, I know it must hurt, but you need to sit down before you pass out again."

Momma Rosa answered the door and when Shirley walked in, Rosa hugged her. Shirley held on to Rosa for dear life. Shirley then walked into the family room and she and Jalesia hugged one another. Shirley placed her hands on Jalesia's cheeks. She looked deep into her swollen, bloodshot, red eyes.

Shirley spoke just above a whisper,

"Jalesia, Derrick would not want us to hurt ourselves. We need to pull ourselves together. We have one another. God is able to help us through this situation. Come on let's get it together. We need to look at the news and follow the instructions we have been given as far as verifying Derrick's information. They are requesting his date of birth, driver license information, and social security number."

Jalesia pulled away and started to run again. This time Rosa caught her. She pulled Jalesia into her arms and said,

"Lea, you know I love you. You can cry as much as you need to cry, but I am not going to allow you to hurt yourself. I am here for you. Anything you need, I'm here. Mother loves you, and you can release your hurt or your frustrations on me."

Rosa led Jalesia back into the family room. Zephanie turned on the television to CNN news. There was a commercial on. Jalesia asked Rosa to bring her the notepad next to her bed.

At the top of the page it was written in bold print, "FLIGHT #1272, THURSDAY MORNING LEAVING FROM LOUISIANA TO TAMPA AT 6:00 A.M."

Rosa handed the notepad to Jalesia. By this time the news anchor had returned from commercial break and he began,

"The breaking news for this morning, flight # 1272 crashed this morning. Two hundred sixty passengers on board. There are no expected survivors. The plane left Louisiana International Airport at 6:00 a.m., heading for Tampa International Airport. The plane went down in a wooded area. Once the black box has been recovered the investigation will begin. There were no reports that the plane had experienced any difficulties. Suddenly the plane plummeted, and exploded once it hit the ground. I repeat, THERE ARE NO REPORTED SURVIVORS ON BOARD FLIGHT #1272."

Jalesia tilted her head back on the couch and slumped down. She began to cry all over again,

"Mother, it just isn't fair."

Jalesia began to scream,

"DOES ANYBODY HEAR ME? IT JUST ISN'T FAIR. I CANNOT TAKE THIS."

Jalesia stood up and made another break to run. Zephanie caught her before she could get away. Zephanie's voice was stern, but yet sympathetic. She placed her hands on Jalesia's shoulders. She looked into her eyes and said,

"Listen Jalesia, you can't do this to yourself. If you don't calm down, you are going to make your self sick."

Jalesia screamed back at Zephanie,

"I DON'T CARE ABOUT GETTING SICK. THE MAN THAT I LOVE IS DEAD. YOU HAVE YOUR HUSBAND."

Jalesia broke free from Zephanie's grip and pointed around the room,

"All of you in this room have the man that you love. I will not be able to look into Derrick's face again. We can't take walks together anymore. I won't hear him say he loves me anymore. All the plans we made in life are over. I can't ever carry his seed. Every part of Derrick Curtis Dubois is over. I am not going to get sick, I am already sick."

Jalesia began to scream again,

" I JUST WANT EVERYONE TO LEAVE ME ALONE. LET ME MOURN. IF I WANT TO CRY, LET ME CRY. IF I WANT TO

SCREAM, JUST LET ME SCREAM. NINE DAYS FROM MY WEDDING DAY, AND THIS HAPPENS."

Jalesia wrapped her arms around her self and cried even harder, "YES, I AM HURTING, AND NO ONE IN THIS ROOM UNDERSTANDS MY PAIN."

Rosa stood up and wrapped her arms around Jalesia as she spoke softly,

"There is nothing wrong with crying or screaming. You can let it all out. We are here for you. We're not trying to tell you what to do. If you want to scream go right ahead."

Zephanie called for a group hug, and prayed a mighty powerful prayer.

She then turned to Jalesia and spoke softly,

"Do you want to lay down to get some rest? I know your head is pounding. I can give you something that will calm you down and help you to rest."

Jalesia gave Zephanie a broken-hearted smile,

"Do you have a pill that will bring Derrick back? I do need something for my headache, and maybe some rest will help."

Jalesia started crying all over again,

"This is unbelievable. I have gone through so much in the past few weeks, but I don't think I can make it through this. The pain is too much to bear. I really, really do love Derrick, and I will never be able to prove my love to him."

Rosa walked Jalesia to her room and helped her into her bed. Zephanie went into the kitchen to get some water for Jalesia to take her pills. Zephanie came back into the room and said,

"J, this pill that I'm giving you will help you to rest for a few hours. I will be here for you. I'm not going anywhere."

Rosa shook her head in agreement,

"Yes baby, me too. I will be right here when you wake up."

Jalesia took the medicine and within five minutes she was asleep. Zephanie and Rosa went back into the family room to talk and comfort Shirley. Shirley stood up when they entered the room, and spoke softly,

"I am going to go home. I wanted to come and see how Jalesia was doing. A week or so ago we had breakfast. We talked about

Derrick for hours. I knew then how much Jalesia loved him. I knew this would shake her up pretty bad. I left my husband and told him I was coming over here to make sure Jalesia was okay. I will need to contact Derrick's siblings to tell them the bad news. Also, I need to call the airlines with Derrick's information that they are requesting."

Rosa walked Shirley to the door, and with a concern look on her face said,

"Shirley, if you need me for anything just let me know. I am here for you and your family. Don't hesitate to call me. I will be here with Jalesia until she can stand to be alone."

Chapter Forty

*R*osa and Zephanie were sitting around talking about how to handle Jalesia when she awakes. Rosa mentioned how they would have to assist with canceling the wedding plans and moving into funeral arrangements. They discussed the fact that Derrick and Jalesia were not married, therefore Derrick's family would probably want to make all the arrangements.

Zephanie's concern was for Jalesia. She asked,

"Mother, what is it for us to do other than pray? I feel so bad for my sister. She has gone through so much lately. The whole rape situation, then she and Derrick had a big pow-wow because she didn't tell him about the rape incident...."

Rosa interrupted with her eyebrows raised and a puzzled look on her face,

"Uh huh! Now I get it. Derrick called me from New York while you all were at dinner. He asked me did Jalesia tell me the whole story. I played dumb, and I never let on that I knew she had been raped. I could sense that Derrick was up to something."

Zephanie agreed,

"Yes, that is right. He was trying to find out if she told you, but did not tell him about her being raped. He found out about it from the news. He felt a little betrayed. She had to deal with that and now he is gone. I talked with her the other night, and she was telling me that they had made up. She was saying how she did not want to be around him now because she did not want to be tempted to make love to him. She was telling me how hard it would be to hold out for the wedding night if she is around him. I told Jalesia that making up is bittersweet. Bitter because you don't want to fight, but sweet because love is so sweet when you have made up. Now we have this situation. In this situation you just don't know what to do. I will just continue to pray, and leave it in God's hand."

Rosa and Jalesia were in the family room. They continued to talk. They turned the television back on to watch some more of the news. On every channel the media was focused on the plane crash.

While watching television, suddenly there was a bump at the door. A key turned and unlocked the door. Out of fear, Rosa and Zephanie jumped up and ran into the bedroom. Zephanie peeped around the corner. She let out a deafing scream,

"AAAAAHHHH! DERRICCCCK, is that you?"

Zephanie ran towards Derrick with her arms extended crying hysterically. Rosa was right behind her also screaming. She had her hand over her heart,

"OH – MY – GOD! DERRICK? THAT IS YOU."

Zephanie and Rosa were now crying uncontrollably. Rosa hugged and squeezed Derrick tightly, and did not want to let him go. Derrick dropped his luggage, fell to his knees, and began to weep like a baby. Derrick spoke through his tears,

"I had been trying to call, but the phone was off the hook. I was at the airport early this morning, and I was on standby. No seats came open in first class. They had one seat available in coach, but I wanted first class for the legroom. I was so excited about getting back home. When Jalesia and I talked last night, I promised her I was going to get out of the habit of having to have things my way. I asked a gentleman to sell me his seat in first class, but every time I thought about purchasing that seat, I could here Jalesia telling me, 'some things money can't buy, stop being impatient, and God will move more in your life'. As much as I wanted to get home early, Jalesia's comments kept ringing in my head. I made up in my mind that I was going to start today being patient and listen to the voice of the Lord. I can truly say that the Lord has spared my life. After I heard about the plane crash, I had been crying, and thanking God every since. I intend to make the best of my life from here on out. On my flight home I have had a lot of things to consider, and I plan to do some things different."

Derrick stood to his feet and wiped away his tears,

"Where is Jalesia? I want to marry her today and make it official next weekend. I thought about if anything were to happen to me, I would not want any questions asked as to whom my belongings would be left to. I will be going today to make her sole beneficiary of every thing I own."

Zephanie interjected as her voice continued to tremble,

"Derrick, you don't have to be married to make out a will. Now, if you just want to get married right away, then you can."

Rosa was still shaking and trembling from the shock of Derrick walking through the door. Zephanie could barley stand as she continued to talk,

"Derrick, I gave Jalesia some medication that calmed her down and she's asleep. The medication will wear off soon, so if you want to try and wake her, you can."

Derrick responded,

"No, what I will do is call my mom and let her know I am alright, because when Jalesia wakes up I want her to be in my arms."

Derrick looked in on Jalesia and quietly walked over to her bed. He knelt down beside the bed and kissed her on the cheek. He brushed her hair with his hand. He looked at the swelling around her eyes as he softly stroked her cheek. After starring at Jalesia for several minutes, Derrick came out of the room to call his mom.

When Shirley picked up the phone Derrick could tell that she had been crying. Her voice cracked as she answered the phone,

"Hello."

"Mom?"

Shirley dropped the phone, and in the background Derrick could hear her screaming,

"THANK YOU JESUS! OH MY GOD! YOU ARE AN AWESOME WONDER! THERE IS NONE LIKE YOU NOWHERE! THANK YOU JESUS! THANK YOU JESUS!"

Shirley picked up the receiver and said,

"Derrick, God is good. I will be right over."

Shirley did not wait for Derrick to respond. She hung up the phone, rushed out the door, and headed for Derrick's house.

Derrick sat on the sofa while he waited for his mom to get there. Rosa sat on one side of Derrick and Zephanie sat on the other side. Rosa leaned over and kissed Derrick on the cheek and said,

"I have never been so happy to see you. Derrick, this will be a day we will never forget. God truly is good. I can't wait for Jalesia to see you."

When Shirley arrived, she rushed in and hugged and kissed Derrick. While crying Shirley said,

"I had a strong suspension that you were still alive. I wanted the airlines to confirm that you were on board flight #1272 before I believed completely. I left all of your information, and they are supposed to call me back."

Derrick lifted up his hands in praise,

"Thank God they will not be able to confirm that I was on that flight."

Shirley was still crying as she spoke,

"I did not call your brother or your sister, because I wanted to be sure. Your stepfather was the only person I told, but before I left the house, I told him the good news."

Derrick stood up and walked towards Jalesia's room,

"I guess everyone that needs to be notified has been, with the exception of Jalesia. I'm going to bring her out here and lay her in my arms so when she wakes up she will know I am all right."

Derrick lifted Jalesia from the bed and carried her in the family room. He sat on the sofa and positioned Jalesia in his arms as if he was holding a baby. Derrick began crying as he rocked Jalesia back and forth. He kissed her softly on the lips.

Zephanie came into the room with a warm towel and knelt down beside Jalesia. She wiped the tearstains from Jalesia's face, where she had cried herself to sleep.

Jalesia began to squirm as Zephanie continued to wipe her face. Jalesia gave a big yawn, and a deep stretch as she barley opened her eyes. She closed her eyes, and then suddenly stretched her eyes wide open. Her body became rigid as she looked directly into Derrick's eyes. Then, when Jalesia spoke her voice was hoarse and soft,

"What happened? Did I die too? Are we in heaven? Did God answer my prayers?"

Jalesia reached up and put her arms around Derrick's neck. The warm tears were running down her face. Jalesia was too weak to cry. She closed her eyes and felt Derrick's face, then, she felt her face. She began to weep,

"Thank you Lord for answering my prayers. Thank you for giving me new life, and for giving me back Derrick. Lord to you, I will be forever grateful."

Jalesia opened her eyes again. Her voice was hoarse when she spoke,

"Sweetheart, please forgive me for not standing and praising God for the great things He has done, but I am extremely weak. I could barely lift my arms."

Derrick began to talk,

"We have been waiting for you to wake up. Our mommas are here, and Zephanie is here also. They have been waiting by your side every since you heard the news."

Derrick bent down and kissed Jalesia softly on the lips. He lifted her up in his arms and held her tenderly. The tears began to flow from Derrick's eyes again,

"I love you, and we will forever be together."

Jalesia wiped the tears from Derrick's eyes and responded,

"I love you too honey."

Jalesia reached for Derrick's head to pull him closer to her again for another kiss,

"Is that the best kiss you can give me? Do you know how many hugs and kisses you owe me?"

Derrick responded,

"Well I was trying to respect our mommas and Zephanie."

Jalesia waved everyone off then commented,

"If they don't understand the kiss that I want right now then they just don't understand. Now kiss me like you miss me."

Derrick gave Jalesia the kiss that she wanted. Shirley, Rosa and Zephanie were applauding.

Jalesia squirmed, sat up on the sofa, and stretched forth her hands to her mom. Rosa walked over and knelt down in front of Jalesia. She hugged her gently and concluded tearfully,

"Truly God has blessed us this day."

Zephanie joined in with the hugs. She put her arms around Jalesia and said,

"From here on I can see things looking up for you. You have been through so much, but I can hear God saying, you have passed the test, and there are brighter days coming."

Jalesia and Zephanie held on to one another and cried together. Zephanie and Rosa moved out of the way as Shirley knelt down between Derrick and Jalesia. She put her hands on both their cheeks and pulled them closer to her, and she spoke through her tears,

"I am truly happy today. God has smiled on me. He has given me back my son, and He's given me another daughter. I could not have asked Him for better. Our families are going to have such a bond that we will feel like one big happy family. All I can say right now is, Thank you Jesus! Thank you Jesus!"

When Shirley got up she told Derrick she was going to leave them alone. She was going home to continue to praise the Lord.

Rosa and Zephanie were gathering up their things so they could also head out the door. While they were walking towards the door Jalesia stopped them and said,

"Mother, Zephanie, please don't leave. I want to take a bath, and I may be too weak to standalone. I wanted to know if you would stay with me while I take my bath?"

Zephanie looked at Jalesia with a smile on her face,

"Are you sure that you don't want Derrick to help you with your bath."

Jalesia smiled back,

"No, I am all the more determined that when Derrick sees me naked, I will be Mrs. Dubois. I have nine days, and after that I could be naked in the kitchen cooking breakfast, and that would be legit."

Rosa responded as she shook her head,

"Not the kitchen. You can pick any other room in the house, but not the kitchen."

They all laughed. Derrick walked Shirley to the door, and Zephanie and Rosa went into the bathroom to assist Jalesia.

Zephanie explained to Jalesia that the medication she had given her was strong, and she may be off balance for a short period of time, but it will eventually wear off.

Chapter Forty-one

*D*errick and Jalesia was finally alone. Derrick was sitting on the sofa with Jalesia in his arms. Jalesia was gaining her strength, even though her voice was still hoarse when she spoke,

"So Derrick, tell me what happened this morning."

Derrick explained to Jalesia how there were no more seats on the plane, except for one middle seat in coach. He explained how he hates coach because he never has enough legroom.

"I thought long and hard about getting on that plane. My mind was on how much I wanted to see you. But I thought about how you were telling me to be nice, because money can't buy me everything. While I was standing there contemplating about purchasing that seat in coach, I asked a gentleman did he want to sell his seat in first class. I then told the man that I would wait for the flight that I was scheduled for. I left you a message, but its obvious that you did not get it. After I heard about the plane crash, I tried several times to call, but the phone was off the hook."

Derrick sat Jalesia up, walked over to the answering machine, and replayed the message.

"You have one message, beeeep, 'Hi Sweetie, I know you are asleep. I am still at the airport and a little angry. I was hoping for that early morning flight, so I could get back home. I'm trying to be Mr. Nice guy like you wanted me to be. I could have bought me a seat in first class and made someone else move. I remembered you telling me to learn how to be patient, and stop thinking that money could buy me every thing. Well, I have been here since four-thirty a.m., and if this is not learning how to be patient, I don't know what is. I guess I will catch the next flight. Don't expect me to be home until late afternoon. I will see you when I get there. I can't wait to get back home. Sweetheart, I love you, and I miss you. Kiss, kiss, kiss, kiss.' Beeeep."

Derrick sat back down on the sofa, and laid Jalesia back down in his lap. He lifted up his hands in praise,

"This is a testimony for me. I am so thankful that the Lord would not allow me a seat on that plane. I guess it was not my time yet. I have so much I need to do now that the Lord has spared my life."

Jalesia looked up at Derrick and said,

"I promise you this day that I will not keep any important information from you. My only thought was that I didn't want to loose you."

Derrick held one finger in the air and put it over Jalesia's lips,

"Sssssh! We don't want to discuss that right now."

Derrick stopped and remembered what Jalesia told him about controlling the conversation.

"I'm sorry. I said I would start allowing you to talk, and get what ever you need off your chest. If you want to discuss the rape incident then we can. Now once we discuss this, we are going to close this chapter of our lives and move forward. We have pressed charges. The man is behind bars for at least thirty years. We have so many good things to look forward to."

Jalesia looked up at Derrick and said,

"All I want to know is, will you see a counselor with me so we can discuss this openly?"

Derrick smiled at Jalesia and said,

"I will do anything your want me to do. Outside from God, I have talked to one of the best counselors in the world. Zephanie and I have talked. I called her one night while I was away, and she told me everything I needed to know. She explained to me her situation, and how important it was for Michael to know what she had experienced when she was raped. Your sister was looking out for you. She explained to me exactly what I needed to do in order for you to experience what making love is suppose to be like. Zephanie and I had a powerful prayer, and the Lord assured me that we have nothing to worry about. Remember our conversation that God has everything under control. Now, need I say more?"

Jalesia started smiling, and she held Derrick's cheek in her hand as she complimented him,

"My husband is the smartest, the finest, the best looking, and the most caring man in the world. I really do look forward to the day when I become your wife. We don't need to go to counseling if you have already talked to Zephanie, because that was going to be my recommendation."

Derrick looked deep into Jalesia's eyes and he did not care if she was exhausted. He had been waiting to kiss her passionately before he left to go to Texas, and he was not going to let this moment pass him by. Derrick and Jalesia passionately kissed one another until they both were panting. After a series of hot passionate kisses, Derrick had to stop. He stood up, straightens his pants, and fixed his shirt. Jalesia sat up and called Derrick back to the sofa,

"What is wrong with you? Come back over here."

Derrick answered,

"I can't keep doing this to myself, turn on, turn off, turn on, turn off. My heart says, Derrick, you can wait. My spirit says, Derrick, you can wait. But sweetheart."

Derrick looked down at his pants,

"Just look at me. My body is not saying Derrick you can wait. My body is screaming, WHAT ABOUT ME!"

Derrick reached for Jalesia's hand and helped her up from the sofa. He pulled her into his arms. Derrick kissed Jalesia softly and said,

"Sweetheart, let's get married today and make it official next Saturday."

Jalesia asked in a jokingly way,

"Why? Are you burning?"

Derrick jokingly answered,

"You know I am burning. I have been burning for a long time, but has that changed anything? On a serious note, I just want to be able to be with you like I want to. Not holding back on anything."

Jalesia hugged Derrick,

"Derrick, you don't have long now. Next Saturday we will be getting married."

Derrick sat back down on the sofa and continued,

"Yes, you're right. Wow! I did not know preparing for a wedding could be so much torture."

Jalesia sat on Derrick's lap. She kicked her heels up on the sofa and crossed her legs at the ankle. She took a deep sigh and looked into Derrick's dark, beautiful eyes. She took her thumb and ran it across Derrick's thin, red, sexy lips. She gently kissed Derrick and said,

"Derrick, you are handsome and every time I look into your eyes, I just get caught up in the moment of how handsome my man is. I was mesmerized the first time I saw you."

Derrick moved Jalesia's hand from his face, and closed his eyes so she would not look deep into his eyes. He then picked Jalesia up and moved her off his lap and said,

"I know what you are doing right now, and it's not fair. I want you to know that my day is coming and pay back is a monster. I know you are teasing me. If you want to talk sexy to me, do not sit on my lap until after we are married."

Jalesia playfully sat back on Derrick's lap and said,

"I can sit on your lap if I want to."

Derrick shrugged his shoulders, wrapped his arms around Jalesia and said,

"Okay, go ahead and sit there, but don't get offended, because I warned you that I am not under control."

Jalesia got up and sat on the chair across the room. Derrick responded,

"I don't care about you sitting across the room, in fact, that may be better. God in heaven knows next Saturday it is on. I am going to see how many games you will be playing with this lap sitting challenge."

Jalesia waved Derrick off,

"Yeah, yeah, yeah, I hear you talking. The proof is in the pudding."

Derrick stood up smiling at Jalesia,

"Go ahead and be bad. I will have my day."

Jalesia stood up and walked towards Derrick with her hands in the air,

"Okay Superman, you win. I'm just having a little fun. I know you got it going on."

Jalesia changed to a more serious conversation,

"Derrick, let's not forget Saturday is our wedding rehearsal, and next Thursday night is our dinner rehearsal. Our schedule is going to be really busy. Tomorrow is Friday and I want to go to church with Mother. Would you go to church with me on tomorrow? I feel we need to be praising the Lord for all the great things He has done."

Derrick wrapped his arms around Jalesia, and squeezed her closely and said,

"Of course, I will go to church with you tomorrow night. I must get my praise on. God has been so good to me. Every time I have an opportunity to go into the house of the Lord, I will be there. The wedding is going to be beautiful. I wish you would not worry so much. Your sister has put things together really well. I did not want you doing a lot. That is the reason why we hired your sister. Believe me, she is not doing this for free. I told her I wanted her best service. She wanted to coordinate this wedding as her gift to you. I told her to give you another gift, because I wanted to pay her for putting this wedding together. Now, if you let her do her job, she will set things in order."

Derrick took Jalesia by the hand, and they walked into the bedroom. He took some papers from his briefcase and snapped his finger,

"Sweetheart, speaking of setting things in order, I really want a sit down reception dinner. Dianiece said that you wanted the reception to be buffet style, because it is less expensive. She gave me a price list on what it will cost to rent the china, glassware, and tableware. Sweetheart, I will only get married one time, and I want my only time to be right. I prefer to sit down and be served. When Dianiece came to me, I was in total agreement with her idea. I told her to make it happen. Also keep in mind that this is when I was upset with you. I felt that I did not need you approval. Now, I want to make sure we are in agreement with one another. I don't want to cut cost on this wedding. I want to pull out all stops, because like I said, I only plan to do this once in my life."

Jalesia picked up the phone and dialed Dianiece number. Dianiece answered the phone,

"Hello."

"Hey, Di, it's me, Lea. Derrick and I were talking about the reception. We decided we would do the sit down dinner."

Dianiece had a surprised tone in her voice,

"You have got to be kidding me. Are you all talking about your wedding, after what you have been through today?"

Jalesia answered,

"We are talking about the wedding, because we are discussing how we plan to spend the rest of our lives together."

Dianiece responded,

"That is beautiful. I'm glad you and Derrick had that discussion. I have already rented the things I will need for your reception. When Derrick told me money was not an object, I knew what I was working with. I realize this is your wedding, but I know what my baby sister wants."

Jalesia and Dianiece continued to talk for about thirty minutes when finally Jalesia explained to Dianiece she had to go, so she could make a call to Otis Jr.

Jalesia was lying across the bed, and Derrick lay opposite of her, as he watched and admired her beauty. When Jalesia got off the phone, Derrick zoomed in for another kiss. Derrick pulled Jalesia in his arms and led off with another round of hot passionate kisses. He then responded,

"For a moment there I thought I was being ignored."

Jalesia rested her hand on Derrick's cheek,

"I will never ignore my sweetie. I want to call Otis Jr. because he is upset that I have not called him to give him an update. You already know that everybody babies me. Do you mind if I call Otis? If you do, you know I will not call him.

"Sweetheart, you know I am only kidding. Of course, I want you to contact your family to let them know how you are doing."

Jalesia dialed Otis Jr. number and her niece answered the phone,

"Sweet pea, where is your dad?"

"He is in his room. I will get him for you, because he is mad at you."

Jalesia asked,

" Mad, for what?"

"He said that you don't call him, and you know he has been worried about you."

"Girl, put your daddy on the phone. I know how to deal with him."

Otis came to the phone,

"Hello."

"Is my big brother mad at me?"

"I am not mad at cha, I just wish you would call people, when you know they're worried about you. When you went to New York, and that man kicked your butt, you withheld that from me. And Mother called me early this morning telling me that your fiancé had died in a plane crash. You should know to let people know how ya doing."

Jalesia was speaking in her apologetic voice,

"I am so sorry. Mother told me that she would call everyone and tell them what had happened."

Otis responded,

"I did hear from Mother, but I wanted to hear from you. Are you so busy now that you can't call your brotha?"

"I said I'm sorry. I will do better. Now, will you forgive me?"

"Okay, I forgive you. Put red-man on the phone, because I know he's sitting right in your face."

Jalesia handed the phone to Derrick,

"Hello?"

"What's up man, this is O. I heard about you, and how God spared your life. Man I'm happy for you. God knows how to get our attention, and keep us on the low. I just wanted to holla at ya, to let you know I thank God for what He has done in this family. Man, you have to take care of yourself, because Lea is a crybaby. I can't stand it when she cries. I'll talk with ya later. Take good care of my sister man."

Derrick concluded the conversation,

"You have nothing to worry about, I will take good care of her. I plan to do everything humanly possible to make her happy. Thanks man for your concern. You are right, God has truly been good to us, and I plan to make the most of my life for Him."

"Alright, it will be later."

"Later Man."

When Derrick got off the phone, he and Jalesia began talking about how good God has been. They said a prayer and began praising God, for the great things He has done.

Derrick looked at Jalesia and said,

"These are the times when you get that strength to press on, and do what is right. I am looking forward to seeing where God is taking you in ministry."

Jalesia responded,

"Don't be surprise, it could be you that He's moving towards ministry. You have a lot He has taken you through, and everything we go through is for a reason. I told you to stretch out and let God take control."

Derrick looked at Jalesia with a sincere look, then began smiling,

"The ministry is in you, and I told you I support you one hundred percent. You have an awesome call on your life, and do not let anyone cause you to retreat, because you're a woman. I am not insecure. The Lord has already taught me everything I need to know about you and your ministry. Sometimes people are insecure about women in ministry, but you don't have to worry about me. The Lord never has to spank me again."

Jalesia hugged Derrick firmly and said,

"Thank you for understanding. Together we are going to make an awesome team."

Jalesia snapped her finger and spoke to Derrick in an apologetic voice,

"Sweetheart I am extremely sorry, but I need to make one more phone call. I had asked Sharon to be my Matron of Honor, and she really did not want to. However, she opted to be a hostess. I will respect her wishes, even though I wanted her to play a bigger role in my wedding. Every since I knew the meaning of best friend Sharon has been there. I realize we walk from two different life styles, but she will always be my friend."

Derrick hugged Jalesia and kissed her on the cheek, then commented,

"I have always said that is why you are so special, because you are real. By all means, call your friend and get things handled."

Jalesia called Sharon and they talked for about fifteen minutes. Sharon was thanking Jalesia for introducing her to JESUS. She shared with Jalesia how her life has turned around and how much she loves the Lord. The tears were falling from Jalesia's eyes as Sharon shared with her that if it was not for Jalesia introducing her to JESUS she don't think she would be alive today.

Chapter Forty-two

*I*t is Thursday morning, two days prior to the wedding day. Zephanie, Jalesia, Sharon and Dianiece were packing all of Jalesia's belongings to move them to Derrick's house once and for all. They knew they had a busy day ahead of them, but they wanted to complete the move first.

Jalesia called Derrick's sister, Paula, to see if she wanted to hang out with them. But since Paula had arrived in town the night before, she may not want to come along. However, after Jalesia called Paula, she was excited about hanging out with the girls.

The girls had planned to spend the day at the spa, getting a massage, a manicure, and a pedicure. It was a day that would be filled with pampering.

Zephanie called Rosa,

"Mother, we are going to be pampered today and hanging out for a little while. Would you like to come along?"

Rosa answered with excitement,

"I sure would! Call Shirley to see if she wants to come along. I know I would love to come along, even if she doesn't want to."

Zephanie called Shirley and she answered the phone,

"Hello."

"Mrs. Shirley, this is Zephanie. Do you want to go to the mall and the spa with us today? Mother is coming and she wanted me to call you and invite you along."

Shirley answered,

"I would love to come along, but I have so much to do today. I will have to take a rain check, but you girls go ahead without me and have fun."

After being pampered the girls hung out at the mall, shopping, eating, and having fun. And while at the mall they decided to go to the movies. After the movie it was late and everyone needed to get home, to get dressed for the dinner rehearsal. Zephanie drove everyone to her prospective destinations.

Jalesia went with Zephanie to her house.

Jalesia would be staying with Zephanie until after the wedding, and Michael would be staying with Derrick until after the wedding.

When Zephanie and Jalesia arrived at the dinner rehearsal they were intentionally late. Rosa was the first to come over to greet Jalesia. Rosa was smiling. She put her arm around Jalesia's waist, kissed her on the cheek, then whispered in her ear,

"That's my girl. You are the highlight of the evening, and you are supposed to make the grand entry. I am sure there were some people, like Derrick, that was a little nervous, but that is how it is suppose to be done."

Jalesia whispered back in Rosa's ear,

"I can't take the credit for being late, because I wanted to be on time. Zephanie held me up. She would not tell me what she was doing and why she wanted to be late."

Rosa softly smiled at Jalesia, rubbed her on the back, and then winked at Zephanie.

Derrick walked towards Jalesia with his hands in his pockets. He was wearing a long sleeve white shirt, a pair of black pleated dress pants, and black suede shoes. Derrick stood in front of Jalesia and starred. He had not seen nor talked to Jalesia since Sunday after church. He then moved closer and whispered in her ear, his voice was deep and sexy,

"You are beautiful, and I miss you terribly. I have to admit, you had me a little worried. However, the next time I am with you, you will be coming down the isle to be Mrs. Dubois."

Jalesia whispered back to Derrick,

"You are so handsome, and God knows you are fine. I have

missed you too. I am excited about the next time we meet. I can hardly wait to be Mrs. Derrick Dubois."

Derrick put his arms around Jalesia and they hugged one another. All eyes were on them. After the hug, Derrick gave Jalesia a soft wet kiss. The wedding party began applauding them. Derrick turned to the guest and escorted Jalesia into the church.

Jalesia sat down in front of the church to watch the flow of the rehearsal. As Derrick was walking back towards the men, he was licking his lips, and rubbing his palms together. He smiled and said,

"This is antagonizing, but I'm enjoying this."

Derrick's brother, Robert, responded,

"All of this drama makes the love better."

Pastor Hamilton came in and prayed over the rehearsal. The entire evening went smooth. Everyone was ready, in place, and did exactly what they were expected to do. Jalesia was crying on and off throughout the evening.

After rehearsal, the wedding party met in the church annex for dinner. Derrick's mom catered the food. She had her staff to serve the guest.

Pastor Hamilton blessed the food, and before they ate, Jalesia had something to say. She stood and faced the guest with tears in her eyes as she began to speak,

"Everyone, I... Excuse me..."

Jalesia stopped in mid sentence and reached for Derrick's hand. He stood beside Jalesia and wrapped his arm around her waist. Jalesia continued to speak,

"We would like to say thank you. You all have worked extremely hard with us to make the beginning of our years together a success. You all are the ones that will make our wedding a success on Saturday. We are grateful, and once again we want to say thank you. All of you know the things Derrick and I have gone through with the plane crash situation, but to God be the glory for the great things He has done. This dinner is a small appreciation from both of us to you. Before we eat, I just feel led to ask my brother, Otis Jr., to stand, and ask everyone to join us while he prays for those families that lost a love one in the plane crash."

After Otis finished praying, Derrick spoke,

"Thank you again. Everyone there is plenty of food, so eat until you are full. Please enjoy yourselves completely."

After Derrick and Jalesia had finished dinner, Derrick was all up in Jalesia's face. He was giving her short sweet kisses when Zephanie walked up to their table smiling. She took Jalesia by the hand and turned to Derrick and said,

"Derrick, you might want to say your goodnights now because the bride to be will be leaving in a few minutes."

Derrick had a surprised look on his face and he asked,

"What do you mean getting ready to leave? The people are not done yet."

Zephanie answered,

"I know the people are not done, but Jalesia has already over stayed her time. I realized you two had not seen one another since Sunday, so I gave her some extra time to be with you, but she will be leaving shortly. Again, you may want to say good night because she will be leaving in a few minutes."

Michael walked up to the table and said to Derrick,

"Derrick, I forgot to tell you about this part. The bride is extra special and she gets the royal treatment. She leaves you looking like a sad puppy dog. But remember what you said about this being a little antagonizing, and that you are starting to enjoy it… Don't worry, the brothers knows how you feel right now, but your day is Saturday."

Rosa, Dianiece, and Zephanie were standing at the table to escort Jalesia off. Jalesia stood and put her hands on Derrick's cheeks and softly kissed him on the lips,

"Love you Booh."

Derrick responded in disappointment,

"Yeah, I love you too."

Chapter Forty-three

*J*alesia and Zephanie hung out together all day Friday. Zephanie was driving her burgundy Lincoln Navigator. They were shopping for lingerie for the honeymoon. They picked out several types from bold tiger print to soft lace and feathers.

Derrick was preparing for his big evening, the day before his wedding day. He was discussing his plans with his brother; Robert, Derrick's best man; two of his ushers; Chris and Tashon, his sister's husband; Kendall, Zephanie's husband; Michael, his soon to be brother-in-laws; Otis Jr. and Edward.

Michael had already planned the evening agenda. They would be getting together later to play spades and doing men things. Michael knew that they would be doing a lot of "tripping" and letting Derrick know the realities of being married.

In the meantime, Zephanie and Jalesia went out to dinner to an expensive steak restaurant. They were talking and enjoying dinner. A few of the Tampa-Bay Buccaneers football players were there. Neither Zephanie nor Jalesia was the least bit interested, even though throughout the night different ones would approach them for conversation.

After eating, Zephanie paid for dinner, and they left the restaurant. Zephanie was driving through traffic as they turned up the volume on the stereo. They were singing loud and Zephanie was using the steering wheel as her drum. She was tapping on the steering wheel and rocking back and forth enjoying their gospel music.

Once they arrived at Zephanie's house, they began putting away their things. Zephanie had Jalesia's suitcase already packed. All she had to do was to add the lingerie to the suitcase. Jalesia sat on the bed and watched Zephanie put her things away.

Jalesia asked, smiling and dangling her feet off the side of the bed,

"Where am I going for my honeymoon? Derrick already told me that you and Michael's gift to us is a paid honeymoon. I know you have already made all the arrangements, so you can tell me where we are going."

"Yes, that is correct, but I will not tell you where you are going. I want it to be a surprise. My job is to make your trip as smooth as possible. I have packed everything you will need. The first two days you will not be wearing much of anything. But after that you will feel sexy, and you will probably want to model some of your nice lingerie."

Zephanie closed the suitcase, took Jalesia by the hand, and walked her back into the family room,

"Come on, let's go in here so we can talk about real stuff."

The two of them went into the family room and were sitting on the floor. Zephanie reached for Jalesia's hand and said,

"Babe, when Derrick makes love to you the first time…"

Jalesia interrupted,

"Zephanie, Derrick and I have already discussed what you talked to him about. He promised me that the first time he makes love to me my toes would curl. Girl, he gave you your props. He said he had one of the best counselors in the world aside from God. I know I am going to be fine, and I can hardly wait."

Jalesia wrung her hands together and said,

"Well, tomorrow is the moment of truth. This is the day I have been waiting for, all of my life."

Zephanie began laughing and said,

"When you walk down the isles tomorrow, let me help you to keep from crying. This is what you do. I want you to look at your pastor and imagine him with dress socks, hard bottom shoes, and running down the beach with a thong. I promise you will not cry, unless you are crying from laughing so hard."

Zephanie lifted her hand to Jalesia for a high five. They then laughed out of control just thinking about what Zephanie had said. They continued talking, laughing, and having girl talk on and off throughout the night.

When the phone rang it startled both Jalesia and Zephanie, but Zephanie allowed the answering machine to pick up. It was Michael. He sounded a little upset when he spoke,

"Zephanie, if you are home please pick up the phone. The only thing I want to do is make sure you and Jalesia has made it home safely. You have Derrick worried. This man can't even enjoy himself for thinking about Jalesia. He wants to make sure she is safe."

Michael's tone became demanding as he continued,

"Zephanie, as your husband I am going to ask you to call me back when you hear this message. If I don't hear from you within five minutes I will come over and set some things in order."

Zephanie looked at Jalesia and smile,

"I am so glad I know my husband, because he is just showing off. I promise you after he left that message he rose up to the brothers, told them that he had spoken, and that I would call him back within the next five minutes."

Jalesia looked at Zephanie as if she had all the answers to life situations and asked,

"What are you going to do?"

Zephanie responded,

"I will stroke his ego and give him what he wants. But first I will wait for at least ten minutes. That way Michael will know that I'm aware of the game that he is playing. You know, men like to show off in front of their friends. One way of showing off is to look like they are in control. When your man is good to you, like my man is to me, I don't care about making him look like he wants to look in front of his friends. I will do anything for my husband and I know he will do anything for me. That is why our marriage has lasted, because I know how far to push Michael, and he knows how far to push me. We don't have many heated discussions because we have learned how to pray, and not discuss certain matters if we have to yell and scream about them."

Zephanie waited for ten minutes then she called Derrick's house. Derrick answered the phone,

"Hello."

"Derrick, may I speak with Michael?"

Derrick sounded sad,

"Zephanie, that was Michael calling for me. I wanted to see if Jalesia was all right. I don't want to talk with her, I just wanted to make sure that you all had made it home safely."

Zephanie answered,

"Derrick, we are fine. We're just laughing, talking, tripping, and getting ready for tomorrow. Would you like to speak to Jalesia? She is standing right here."

Derrick got happy and said,

"Yes! Sure, I would love to speak with her."

"I will put her on the phone, but before I do, may I please speak with Michael for a minute?"

Michael came to the phone with, the big head, and his chest stuck out,

"What's up babe? Thanks for doing what I asked of you."

Zephanie replied,

"I just wanted to tell you that you can deflate your head, and I love you."

Michael was still showing off and said,

"Well, as long as you know which side the bread is buttered on."

Zephanie spoke with a more sincere tone,

"Michael, put Derrick back on the phone, and don't show off too much. You know you are the man. I love you."

"Love you too. Bye."

Michael handed the phone to Derrick and Zephanie handed the phone to Jalesia.

Jalesia spoke with a soft sexy voice,

"Derrick, do you miss me?"

"Yes sweetheart, I do miss you. Do you miss me?"

"I sure do. Just think, in less than twenty-four hours we will be married. I can't wait to walk down the isles to spend the rest of my life with you."

Derrick's smile was from ear to ear,

"Aaaaah, yes! I like the way that sounds. I guess I can go back in here and play some spades with the fellas, now that I know my sweetheart is alright."

Jalesia paused for a moment,

"Derrick, I want our marriage to be like no other. If we remember what Pastor Hamilton said. If we keep an open communication and remember, 'Love Is What It Does', then we can accomplish anything. I love you."

"I love you too. Good night."

"Good night, sweetheart."

After Jalesia got off the phone, Zephanie had prepared her a nice hot bubble bath in the Jacuzzi tub. Zephanie smiled at Jalesia and said,

"When you have completed taking a relaxing bath, you should get in the bed, so you will be well rested for tomorrow. You have absolutely nothing to worry about. Everything is in order for tomorrow."

Jalesia walked over and kissed Zephanie on the forehead,

"You are truly a sister. Thanks for everything."

"You are more than welcome. Wait until you see how beautiful this wedding is going to be. The honeymoon will speak for itself."

Chapter Forty-four

The wedding day, that Saturday afternoon, has finally arrived. Zephanie and Rosa is Jalesia's support beam. They all met with the hair stylist and the make-up professional across the street from the church at the annex. It was time for Jalesia to start getting ready for the wedding. The church annex was closed off from everyone except for Jalesia's immediate personnel. Dianiece met Jalesia, and Zephanie at the annex to explain a few things to them. She wired an earphone walkie-talkie to Zephanie. Zephanie would be the contact person in the bride's party. Michael would be the contact person in the groom's party. All hostesses were wired along with Dianiece.

Dianiece explained to Zephanie that if Jalesia needed anything, to contact her personally, and not to go through any one else. She explained that they had four cameramen. One will be stationed in the bride's dressing room, one in the groom's dressing room, one at the front entrance outside the church, and one inside the church. After the wedding begins all the cameramen will come inside and position themselves to complete the recording.

There was a giant screen set up in the annex so Jalesia could watch the inside of the church as the different ones entered the sanctuary.

Dianiece looked at Jalesia and said,

"Sister, you are beautiful. Everything is under control. Take your mind off everything else and focus on Jesus and Derrick. This is your day, and you are not to worry about anything. You have trusted me up to this point, so continue to trust me. Everything will be just the way you want it to be."

Dianiece took Jalesia and Zephanie by the hand and said a prayer. After she had finished praying, she hugged Jalesia and reaffirmed everything she had said.

Pastor Hamilton was already at the church in his office. The crowd had started gathering. The musician and soloist were already in place. In front of the church, there was a half circle driveway for a drop off point. The first sets of doors were glass doors and the second set was wood. If the wood doors were opened, you would be able to see from the pulpit to the front door.

Derrick and his crew had finally arrived. They pulled in front of the church in a white stretched limo and a white Cadillac Escalade. The men in the wedding party knew they would not be riding in the limo after the wedding. They knew to bring the Cadillac so that they would have transportation to the reception.

The ushers were dressed in black tuxedos, burgundy cummerbunds and burgundy bow ties. The hostesses had on off white dresses with gold embroidery. The bridesmaids had on burgundy satin gowns with burgundy matching shoes, and gold accessories.

Michael was not in the wedding party, but he was the man that was assigned to keeping everything in order for Derrick. He too had on his black tuxedo, burgundy cummerbund and burgundy tie.

When Dianiece saw Michael, she wired him with a microphone. Michael's assignment was Derrick. Whatever Derrick wanted or needed, Michael was to be there.

Derrick and his best man, Robert, went into Pastor Hamilton's office. While they were inside, Michael stood outside the office doors. Pastor Hamilton prayed with Derrick and Robert. After the prayer, Derrick asked,

"Is Jalesia here yet?"

Pastor Hamilton smiled and answered,

"Oh yes, she has been here for hours getting dressed."

Derrick went to the door and asked Michael to step inside. He said with a concern look on his face,

"Michael, would you asked them if Jalesia is ok?"

Michael spoke into the microphone,

"Zephanie, I am in the Pastor's Office with Derrick. He wants to make sure Jalesia is okay."

Zephanie responded,

"Please let Derrick know everything is going according to plan."

Zephanie paused,

"Tell Derrick, Jalesia said she loves him, and she will show her love for him in a matter of minutes."

Michael told Derrick what Jalesia said. Then, he walked back out the door as Derrick breathed a sigh of relief.

The people were still filing in, and Pastor Hamilton looked down at his watch and said,

"Well gentlemen, it is time for us to take our places."

Derrick put his hand on his stomach,

"Man, the knots in my stomach are twisting and turning. I am suppose to do a surprise song presentation to Jalesia, but I don't know if I can do it."

Robert placed a hand on Derrick's shoulder,

"Bro, you are going to do just fine. Stop worrying about things. Jalesia loves you as much as you love her. I know she can't wait to get this all over, because she is probably just as nervous as you are."

Pastor Hamilton put his hand on Derrick's shoulder and said under the anointing,

"We have prayed, and I believe God will make everything all right. Besides, when you make that special presentation, Jalesia will run down the isle. Gentlemen, shall we do this?"

Derrick, Robert, and Pastor Hamilton were standing down front. Robert was dressed in a black tuxedo with a gold cummerbund and bow tie. Derrick was dressed in an off-white, long tail tuxedo with a burgundy cummerbund and bow tie, which had gold embroidery running through them. Pastor Hamilton had on an off white robe with a burgundy and gold stole.

Both sets of the doors were open and Derrick could see everyone that came up.

The bride's maids and ushers started filing in one by one, as they took their respective places.

The carriage was waiting across the street at the annex. Rosa was the first one to be brought over to the main sanctuary in the carriage. And when the carriage pulled in front of the church, Rosa stepped out. The usher escorted her down the isle, and Rosa lit the candle as she had rehearsed. Then, Rosa was escorted to her seat.

Jalesia was in the annex and she could see everything that was going on inside the sanctuary from the giant screen. When she saw her mother walking down the isle, she started fanning, trying to prevent the tears from falling.

Shirley then walked in, escorted by her husband. She lit the candle as she had rehearsed. Afterwards, she was escorted to her seat.

The carriage went back to the annex to pick up Zephanie, who was the maid of honor. After the carriage arrive to take Zephanie to the main sanctuary, she then turned to Jalesia and said,

"I am going to leave now, because it's my time to take my walk. You are beautiful, and I have to admit, today only, you look better than me."

Jalesia eyes were filled with tears as she spoke,

"Zephanie, how can I say thank you? You are here for me once again."

Zephanie answered,

"You have been there for me, so I could ask you the same question, but I already know the answer. That's what friends are for. Hey, don't forget what I said, think of your pastor standing in front of you with his dress socks and wearing a thong."

They both laughed, and Jalesia was able to fight back her tears. Zephanie walked out and instructed the hostess exactly what to do. She told the hostess to make sure everything was in order with Jalesia when she steps off the carriage.

The carriage took Zephanie across the street to the main sanctuary. Jalesia watched the big screen as Zephanie walked slowly down the isle.

Zephanie was beautiful. She was dressed in an off-white gown, with gold accessories. The gown had gold embroidery running through it. Her hair was in an up-style. She looked flawless, and every thing was in place.

After Zephanie took her place, the usher rolled back the runner and closed the sanctuary doors. The flower girls stood prepared to come down the isle to drop the rose petals. Otis senior took his place half way up the isle.

Derrick was handed a cordless microphone. He then looked directly into the camera, and sung a romantic song to Jalesia that he had written. Derrick poured his heart and soul into the song. And when he was finished the people were standing to their feet applauding.

Jalesia was watching the monitor, and she began to cry. She never knew Derrick could sing. She was not expecting this special presentation, and was stunned to hear Derrick sing so well.

Jalesia's make-up artist was there to refresh her make up before she got in the carriage. Afterwards, Jalesia was taken across the street to the main sanctuary. Once Jalesia arrived at the main sanctuary, the hostess made sure everything pertaining to Jalesia was in order.

Soft music was playing as the flower girls walked down the isle dropping rose petals. After the flower girls took their place, everyone in the room was standing watching the door, waiting for Jalesia to come through.

When the double doors were finally opened, Jalesia stepped into the sanctuary. She was beautiful. She stood still for a moment before she began to walk slowly down the isle.

The music was playing softly, and Pops was waiting to escort Jalesia to the altar. Her dress was beautiful, white satin and lace. The lace had crosses throughout. The train was Seventeen feet long. Every strand of her hair was in place. She was wearing her hair in cute candy curls. The veil had an open top to it.

Derrick's eyes were glued to Jalesia as she walked down the isle. Derrick was standing with his finger intertwined behind his back as he rocked a little and continued to lick his luscious red lips.

When Jalesia eyes finally met up with Derrick's eyes, she did not turn away. Jalesia's only thought was on how handsome Derrick looked. His facial hairs were trimmed the way she likes them.

When Jalesia met Otis, she placed her hand in the bend of his arm as he escorted her the remainder of the way. When they reached the end of the isle, Pastor Hamilton asked,

"Who will give Jalesia Anna Brantz away?"

Otis held up one finger,

"Pastor Hamilton, I do, O.T. Brantz, Sr."

Otis lifted Jalesia's veil, and kissed her softly on the lips. He then placed Jalesia's hand in Derrick's hand.

Derrick looked deeply into Jalesia's soft brown eyes and motioned with his mouth,

"I love you."

Jalesia whispered,

"I love you too,"

One tear rolled down Jalesia's cheek.

Pastor Hamilton was talking, while Derrick and Jalesia were whispering back and forth to one another.

Derrick whispered to Jalesia,

"Don't cry. This is it. You will soon be my wife."

Jalesia was shaking as she responded,

"Derrick, I am so nervous. I'm shaking."

Derrick squeezed her hand,

"Don't be nervous. I am right here. What can I do to make it better?"

Jalesia answered,

"You can't."

Jalesia closed her eyes and looked up.

Pastor Hamilton said with a smile on his face,

"I hope this is not how you two plan to be in church, talking while the Pastor is talking."

The crowd all laughed. Derrick and Jalesia had a moment to smile. The laughs helped Jalesia to get over her crying moment.

Pastor Hamilton walked Derrick and Jalesia through their marriage vows. They went through the ring ceremony and the lighting of the unity candle. When they came to the altar, after lighting the unity candle, Pastor Hamilton had them to kneel, and he prayed an anointed prayer over their lives. Then, Pastor Hamilton had them to stand and face one another and he said,

"By the power of God invested in me, I now pronounce you Husband and wife."

He turned to Derrick and said,

"You may kiss your bride."

Derrick lifted the veil, but he did not kiss Jalesia lightly on the lips as they had rehearsed. Instead, he gave her a full mouth long kiss, and when he did, the Ooooohs and Aaaaahs erupted throughout the sanctuary.

Pastor Hamilton had them to face the congregation and he said,

"Listen here, after that kiss, don't you all bother this couple while they are on their honeymoon."

The congregation laughed.

Pastor Hamilton continued,

"Everyone, I present to you Mr. and Mrs. Derrick and Jalesia Dubois."

Once again the applause were throughout the sanctuary.

Zephanie was working hard on keeping Jalesia's train spread out. Derrick and Jalesia walked up the isle and out the door to an awaiting limousine.

Jalesia got into the Limo and Derrick followed afterwards. Once Derrick got inside the limo, he locked the doors, and close off the middle partition. The driver had already been given instructions not to be the first one to the convention center for the reception.

While riding in the limo, Derrick was kissing all over Jalesia. Derrick jokingly said,

"Take off all your clothes now."

Jalesia turned her back to Derrick and said,

"Unzip my dress, and I will."

Derrick responded,

"See, I know not to play with you, because you will do it."

"Why not? You are my husband, and marriage is honorable right?"

Derrick continued kissing Jalesia, and while still laughing, joking and playing with her he grabbed her breast and continued,

"I have been waiting on this day for a long time, but I will not start nothing I can't finish. I know we are heading over to the reception, and I don't want to get all worked up in my body, so I am going to leave you alone."

Jalesia continued playing with Derrick where he left off. She playfully grabbed a handful of his crouch and said,

"That's right, don't start nothing you can't finish. I have been waiting for a long time to grab this crouch, so I can see if all of this is real."

Derrick eased Jalesia's hand aside and said,

"O.K. Let's stop playing before we get serious. You see, I can't hide myself if I get all worked up, so let's stop playing."

Jalesia's countenance immediately changed to sadness and she said,

"O.K. I will stop playing, but can I at least get a kiss? I need you to help me to take this train off, because it is all in my way."

Derrick smiled warmly and assisted Jalesia in removing the train. Then Jalesia sat on Derrick's lap. She looked straight into Derrick's eyes and kissed him passionately. But right in the middle of the kiss, Jalesia immediately pulled away and retorted,

"Let me tell you how low down you are."

Derrick exclaimed with a surprised tone,

"What did I do?"

"I want to know why did you kiss me, long and hard today, when Pastor Hamilton said you may now kiss the bride?"

Derrick started laughing. Jalesia continued,

"I was expecting this soft kiss, like we had rehearsed, but you totally caught me off guard."

Derrick softly chuckled at Jalesia's line of amusing comments. Then Jalesia casually changed the subject.

"Any way, we had better be heading towards the convention center, do you agree?"

Derrick nodded his head in agreement. He then lowered the partition and asked the chauffer to take them to the Convention Center.

While in route to the convention center, Derrick and Jalesia continued to kiss one another romantically. They were so caught up in the moment that they did not realize when the limo had stopped moving and they were parked directly in front of the convention center.

Chapter Forty-five

ow, once at the Convention Center, a crowd of people was standing outside awaiting their exit from the limo. Rosa, Otis, Zephanie, and Michael were standing at curbside. Then, after the newlyweds exited the limo, they were greeted with many hugs and kisses.

Jalesia and Derrick felt like celebrities as they walked through the crowd of people. After they had passed through the crowd, everyone followed behind them for the reception. Dianiece was holding the microphone to announce the wedding party. Jalesia was impressed with Dianiece, and how she had grabbed the bull by the horns and accepted the duty of coordinating the wedding and the reception. Everything was beautiful and in order just like Jalesia had dreamed it would be.

Dianiece called out the names of all the ushers and bridesmaids. She then announced the brother of the groom, Robert and his wife, Tanisha White, the maid of honor, Dr. Zephanie and husband, Michael Morris. Next she announced the parents of the groom, Mr. and Mrs. Rogers. After that, she announced the bride's parent, who was also her parents, Mr. and Mrs. Otis and Rosa Brantz. Dianiece took a deep breath, extended her hands towards Derrick and Jalesia and said,

"Now ladies and gentlemen we present to you the honorees for this evening, Mr. and Mrs. Derrick and Jalesia Dubois.

The cheers were loud as Derrick and Jalesia took their seats at the head table. Dianiece brought Derrick the microphone and he began speaking with excitement,

"Listen up everyone. The other night I could not do this, but today I can speak for both of us. I want—no, excuse me."

Derrick pointed to himself and Jalesia,

"We want to thank each of you for your support here today, and you will definitely hear from both of us on a later date. Right now, I am going to bring up Pastor Hamilton to bless the food. Afterwards, we will be in the most capable hands of my wonderful sister-in-law, Dianiece. I'm hungry and ready to eat. I have not had an appetite lately, but I have my 'good thing' now and my appetite is back."

Derrick handed the microphone to Pastor Hamilton.

After Pastor Hamilton blessed the food, he passed the microphone back to Derrick.

Derrick addressed the guest once again,

"You will be served tonight and if you want seconds or thirds, please ask. We have plenty of food, and no one should leave here hungry. Before I take my seat, would you put your hands together and help me thank my sister-in-law, Dianiece Precious Brandon. She has worked really hard coordinating the wedding and the reception. I truly thank God for her and her husband. Her husband has allowed her the time to work on this project. Precious, thanks once again, its now in your hands."

The guest applauded Dianiece. She then walked to the head table and gave the waitress and waiters their cue to serve the guest. And the hostesses will serve the head table.

The main entree consisted of your choice of Jumbo fried shrimps with steak, fried chicken with pot roast, or chicken cordon bleu with prime rib. The plates were prepared with a variety of steamed vegetables, mashed potatoes and gravy, green beans, rice pilaf, and fried corn. There were baskets of corn bread, soft rolls, and biscuits. The choices to drink were soft drinks, lemonade, iced tea, or water.

Derrick and Jalesia sat center of the head table, while different ones would come up to their table to congratulate them or to talk. Many people stopped to talk about something, nothing, anything, and everything.

Derrick was eating, but Jalesia did not want anything to eat. Jalesia had her arm around Derrick's chair. He then leaned over to whisper in her ear,

"I think you need to eat, so you can be well nourished."

Jalesia whispered back,

"I am not hungry, and besides I am already well nourished."

Derrick was licking his lips and bobbing his head back and forth,

"O.K., remember I warned you, when you run out of energy, and I keep going, and going, and going…"

Jalesia rested one hand on Derrick's thigh, and with her other hand she stroked his cheek and whispered,

"You are so nasty."

Derrick began laughing and asked,

"Who me? Not me. You are the one who is nasty. I am talking about getting nourishment for the dances that are coming up. Also I am talking about leaving for our honeymoon. And you will need energy for the trip."

Jalesia began laughing. She pushed Derrick's leg and said,

"That is not what you were talking about. I know right now your mind is stuck on love making, and I don't care what your mouth says."

"No, you are wrong. My mind is on our honeymoon. And I am looking forward to where we are going."

Jalesia's mood became more seductive,

"Derrick, tell me, where are we going?"

"I can not tell you. Zephanie would kill me."

Jalesia rested her hand high up on Derrick's thigh,

"If you don't tell me I am going up higher."

Derrick remained calm and cool,

"I am not telling. I don't care how high you go."

Derrick tried to ignore Jalesia's movement up his thigh as he continued to eat his food. When Jalesia touched Derrick's crouch, he did not flinch,

"I'm still not telling you."

Jalesia was starring at Derrick with her hand on his crouch. When Rosa walked over to the table to congratulate the newlyweds, she startled Jalesia. Jalesia immediately snatched her hand away form Derrick's crouch.

Rosa commented,

Would you get out of the man's face so he can eat? I can see already that when you two come back from your honeymoon, I will have a grandchild on the way."

Derrick responded,

"That will be alright with me."

Jalesia was too embarrassed to respond. She did not know if Rosa saw her with her hand on Derrick's crouch or not. Jalesia stood to hug Rosa,

"Mother, I love you and thanks for everything."

"Thanks for what?"

Derrick interrupted,

"Thanks for giving birth to my fine, beautiful wife, and raising her to be the lady that she is today."

Rosa was blushing,

"Derrick, you are more than welcome, but I did what any mother would do for her daughter."

Derrick was shaking his head no,

"No mother, any mother would not do what you have done, but I thank God for this lady. I plan to make the best of our lives together."

Rosa turned and walked away. Derrick sat with a smirk on his face. Jalesia asked,

"What are you smiling about?"

"I was tripping off your mom saying you would be pregnant when we come back from our honeymoon. I was thinking to myself, if you don't come back pregnant, it would not be because I did not try."

Jalesia eyebrows rose as she said with a smile on her face,

"Not if I don't find out where we are going on our honeymoon."

Derrick quickly told her,

"Hawaii. We are going to Hawaii, because there is no way I will miss out on making love to you because of a dumb secret."

"Ooooo! I am going to tell Zephanie that you told me."

"If you do, I will tell her you made me tell you or else you would hold back on the love making, but I am sure Zephanie would understand."

As the evening progressed the celebrations continued. The toast was made, the cake was cut, and now it was time for the first dance.

Derrick extended his hand to Jalesia for the first dance. All eyes were on them as Jalesia put her arms round Derrick's neck and he put his arms around her waist. He pulled her ever so closely into his arms.

Jalesia whispered in Derrick's ear,

"Please don't dance with me like you kissed me in the sanctuary."

Derrick whispered back,

"Why not? Everyone in here knows that I am deeply in love with you."

As the song drew near a closed, Derrick gave Jalesia a kiss that made her desire more of him. Jalesia playfully fanned her face. Derrick then took Jalesia by the hand and escorted her off the dance floor. Others walked out on the dance floor and began dancing. Derrick and Jalesia took their places back at the head table.

Different ones were still walking up to Derrick and Jalesia congratulating them. Zephanie and Michael also came over to congratulate them. Softly smiling, Zephanie took Jalesia by the hand and said,

"O.K. Derrick, say your good nights, because Jalesia has to leave."

Derrick waved Zephanie off and jokingly said,

"I am not even worried about that tonight. You nor your momma will be able to tear Jalesia away from me tonight."

Jalesia wrapped her hands around Derrick's arm, shaking her head in agreement,

"My husband could not be more right. I longed for this day, and it has finally come. It's like your present sitting under the Christmas tree and you can't wait to open it, but you know you have to wait until Christmas Day."

Zephanie held up her hand to give Jalesia a high five. Her voice was filled with excitement,

"Girl, I know exactly what you mean but have you ever picked up the gift and you just couldn't wait for Christmas morning, but you opened the present and took a peak, then wrapped it back up?"

Jalesia and Zephanie were laughing and hugging one another uncontrollably. Derrick cleared his throat, and with a wide grin on his face said,

"Zephanie, while you are in a laughing mood, let me apologize now. I'm sorry but I told Jalesia where we were going on our honeymoon. I think you need to tell her the rest."

Derrick looked down at his watch,

"If we are going to make our trip, we need to be getting out of here."

Zephanie put her hand on her hips and sucked her teeth at Derrick,

"O.K., I see I can't tell you anything. How would you feel if I told her about your secret?"

Derrick stood up and put his hand over Zephanie's mouth and begged,

"O.K., I'm sorry. I will know how to keep a secret from now on, but she made me tell her. She was talking about withholding the love making, so I had to tell her."

Zephanie moved Derrick's hand from her mouth and said,

"You and I both know there is nothing that will keep Jalesia from making love with you, so you should not have been concerned. But, I am going to forgive you this time."

Derrick grabbed Zephanie and hugged her. Zephanie spoke with excitement,

"Jalesia, Michael and I wanted to give you and Derrick something special, so we purchased the trip for your honeymoon. It is seven days and six nights stay in Hawaii. I love you both and pray God blesses this marriage to be near perfect, if not perfect. Similar to Michael's and mine."

Zephanie handed the tickets to Derrick and kissed them both on the cheek. Michael then hugged both Jalesia and Derrick.

After Jalesia tossed the bouquet and Derrick tossed the garter th   back down at the head table. Dianiece came to the table   microphone as Derrick requested. Derrick spoke,

one, Jalesia and I thank you for your support, and we to stay, but we have to be leaving if we are going to board our flight tonight. We want you all to enjoy yourselves. This place is reserved until Two a.m., and if you go over, Dianiece knows what to do. She has not been shy about spending our money, and I am sure she will continue if need be. The D.J. is here so let him know what you want. Also I believe Dianiece has a special guest for you on this evening. I pray you all have enjoyed your evening and continue to have fun."

Derrick and Jalesia got into the limo, headed for home to change clothes.

Derrick's cell phone rang. He had no desire to answer the phone but he noticed from the caller id that it was Zephanie,

"Hello."

"Derrick, let me speak to my sister."

"Hold on."

Derrick handed the phone to Jalesia,

"Hello."

"J, I just wanted to tell you that the wedding and the reception was *THE BOMB*. Forget about everything else and focus your attention on Derrick. You two have fun, and I will not call again, unless it's an absolute emergency. If you need me, just call me."

Jalesia responded,

"We are going to be just fine. God has sanctioned this marriage, and can't no devil in hell interrupt God's plan."

Zephanie replied,

"I love you and tell my brother-in-law that I love him too."

"O.K., good-bye."

"Bye-bye."

After Jalesia hung up the phone, she and Derrick started kissing passionately.

Chapter Forty-six

*W*hen the limousine pulled up at Derrick and Jalesia's house, parked in the drive way was a brand new Cadillac Escalade with burgundy exterior and beige leather interior. There was a huge white bow on top of the car. Jalesia put her hand over her mouth and gasped,

"Oh my God! Derrick, is that for me?"

"Yes sweetheart, that is for you. You asked for it, now you have it. I hope you like it."

Jalesia jumped out of the limousine and started dancing around. She then grabbed Derrick by the cheeks and kissed him long and hard.

"Sweetheart, thank you! I love it! I could never repay you for the things you do for me."

Derrick responded,

"Repay? I am not looking for payment. All I want you to be is a good wife."

"Well, I believe I can handle that."

Jalesia and Derrick got into the Cadillac. She was so happy. Jalesia tilted her head back and inhale the smell of new leather. Derrick interrupted her thoughts,

"Honey, I know you want to drive your new car, but we don't have any time tonight. We need to get dressed so we can head to the airport. Our trip is nonrefundable, and Zephanie would kill us if we missed the plane."

Zephanie already had Jalesia suitcase packed and sitting by the door when they arrived. Derrick already had his things ready to go also.

Jalesia walked into the house so she could change clothes. She was in the bedroom undressing when Derrick shouted through the door,

"Sweetheart, I'm going to park the Cadillac in the garage, and pull the Lincoln out front, because I don't want to leave the new car unattended while we're on our trip."

Jalesia ran over and jumped into the bed and then shouted back through the door,

"Sweetheart, come here before you move the vehicles."

Derrick peeped around the corner. Jalesia was lying across the bed with only her bra and panties. She motioned for Derrick to come to her with her index finger.

Derrick walked towards the bed, then stopped,

"What do you want?"

Jalesia's tone was seductive,

"I want you. Come here."

Derrick walked to the foot of the bed then hesitated as he said,

"Sweetheart, you can't have me right now."

Derrick looked down at his watch. Jalesia grabbed Derrick by the arm and pulled him down on the bed and said,

"Okay, but before you go outside, give me a kiss."

Derrick quickly jumped up from the bed. Jalesia stood up and began unbuttoning Derrick's shirt. She then unbuttoned and unzipped his pants and said,

"Derrick, do you need to change your clothes and get out of this tuxedo?"

Derrick stopped Jalesia and looked into her eyes. He could see that Jalesia really wanted him. But he knew he did not have enough time to make love to her like he wanted to, so he said,

"Jalesia, if we are going to board our flight on time, we need to be leaving. I want you as much as you want me, but sweetheart, I want it to be right."

Derrick walked into the closet to get his clothes that he was to wear that night. Jalesia stood in the doorway of the closet to make one last seductive attempt. She looked at Derrick with a very sincere look on her face and said,

"Make love to me."

Derrick rubbed his face with his hands, dropped his shoulders and said,

"I will, but not right now. We don't have time. I don't want a quickie for my first time with you, sweetheart. I want the long, hot, passionate time with you."

Jalesia shrugged her shoulders and dropped her hands to her side. She stepped out of the way so Derrick could get dressed.

Jalesia was sitting on the bed putting on lotion. She had a look of disappointment on her face when Derrick walked into the room naked. Jalesia thought in her mind,

"The nerve of this Negro, to see me in here burning up with desire and he walks his naked butt in the room and totally ignores me."

Derrick did not look Jalesia's way even though he knew that she was watching his every move. Jalesia watched as Derrick put on his string tricot briefs, and she wondered how was he going to put all that masculinity into those small briefs, but somehow he managed. Derrick continued getting dressed. He put on his shiny black pleated pants and his green key knit shirt that was form fitting. You could see his rippling muscles through his shirt. He then put on a sheer buttoned down black shirt over the green key knit shirt.

After Jalesia watched Derrick get completely dressed, she slid into her red form fitting dress and red sandals.

Derrick was waiting in the car. When Jalesia came out of the house, Derrick opened the passenger's door for her. He pulled Jalesia into his arms and pressed his body close to her body. He then lightly kissed her a few times, each time the kiss became more passionate. When Derrick finally unlocked his lips from Jalesia's his voice was husky,

"What happened in the house will never happen again. I will never let you ask me to make love to you, and I not do it. I am sorry. I watched the look of disappointment that you had on your face, and that will never happen again."

Jalesia responded,

"That's okay honey, I should have been able to control my desires and realize we were pressed for time. I am sure we will have plenty of other opportunities. What tripped me out the most, was when you came into the room naked."

Derrick dropped his head in shame and said,

"I'm sorry about that. I was being a little bad. I was trying to make you want me more because I wanted to be on your mind while we're flying in the air."

"Well Derrick, that's called teasing me, but that's alright. It worked. You are definitely on my mind and I can't wait to feel the total man. I hate sounding like this, but I almost feel desperate."

Derrick wrapped his arms around Jalesia again,

"This is exactly what I like. I want you to express yourself to me. It's not that you are desperate. You are showing me how much you love me, and that you are not ashamed of me. I want you as much as you want me, if not more. I am not ashamed to let you know that I want to make love to you. And I don't want you to ever be ashamed to ask me to make love to you. I want to satisfy you in every way. If it's something you want then let me know, and I am willing to explore anything you ask of me. We are now one, and I will make sure you are completely satisfied."

Derrick's stare told Jalesia everything else she needed and wanted to know. She was so caught up in that very moment, that neither of them was aware of the time.

Jalesia held up Derrick's arm and looked at his watch and said,

" I guess we better be going. Look at the time."

Derrick looked down at his watch,

"Oh yes, we better be going,"

Jalesia then zoomed in for one more kiss. This time she led off with the kisses. She softly kissed Derrick on the lips and each time the kiss became hotter and deeper. The feeling Jalesia felt in her body reminded her of the time she and Derrick almost gave in to their desires.

Derrick wrapped Jalesia in his arms and whispered in her ear,

"Today I commit the rest of my life to you. I love you with all my heart."

Chapter Forty-seven

*W*hen Derrick and Jalesia arrived in Hawaii their limousine was waiting. The limo driver drove them to their hotel. The huge, luxurious, penthouse suite had the perfect setting for two people in love. The suite was immaculate. The king size heart shaped bed said *love*, the lights were blinking to the tune of *love*, and everything they looked at said *love*. The balcony over looked the beach. The birds were making soft *love* music. The waves splashing against the beach wall was to the tune of *love*. The nice crisp breeze set the tone for making *love*.

Jalesia had slipped on her soft flowing, red, lace and silk negligee. She was sitting out on the balcony enjoying the cool fresh breeze. She had her heels kicked up as she lies back on the chaise. The cool breeze from the waters below caused Jalesia to close her eyes and meditate on how much she desire to get on with making love with Derrick. She could hardly wait. She knew every moment she waited was worth what she was about to experience. And the wait was almost over.

Derrick came out on the balcony wearing a pair of black satin lounge shorts. He decided not to put on any underwear, shirt, shoes, or socks.

Derrick sat behind Jalesia and pulled her into his arms. He pulled Jalesia's hair up off her neck and softly kissed the back of her neck.

Derrick spoke softly,
"Were you asleep?"
Jalesia quickly answered,
"Of course not. I am sitting here totally relax. I was waiting for you to come out here so I could lay back in your arms."

Derrick stretched his arms above his head, and for a silent moment he thought about how blessed he was. The music from the birds, and the nice crisp breeze, and the splashing of the waters, and to feel Jalesia's body pressed against his body, caused Derrick's temperature to rise. Derrick wrapped his arms around Jalesia and gently cupped her breast.

She closed her eyes and enjoyed the moment of being in Derrick's arms once again. Jalesia could feel Derrick's hard body as he pressed against her body and held her closely. They began to kiss passionately. Derrick lifted Jalesia from the chaise and carried her into the bedroom. He laid her gently on the bed. He completely undressed her and admired her beauty. Derrick stepped out of his lounge shorts, and joined Jalesia in the bed.

Derrick made love to Jalesia, and she never thought about any past experiences. There was nobody but Derrick Curtis Dubois in the room with her, and he made her forget about everything else except how good she was feeling at that very moment. The feeling was…

"Love Is What It Does."

Conclusion

L-O-V-E

*L*ove is a four-letter word that people throw around with the greatest of ease, but does one really know what true love means? A parent can say they love their child, but is it true love if that parent is nowhere to be found? A child can say they love their parents, but is it true love if disrespect and dishonor abound? And what about that spouse that confesses love for their mate? Is it true love when that so called love turns into hate? What is true love?

John 3:16 says, "For God so loved the world, that he gave his only begotten Son, that whosoever believeth in him should not perish, but have ever lasting life." And Romans 5:8 says, "But God commendeth his love toward us, in that, while we were yet sinners, Christ died for us." And John 15:13 says, "Greater love hath no man than this, that a man lay down his life for his friends."

So what is true love? **LOVE IS WHAT IT DOES**.

Acknowledgements

*L*aura Ann Hargrove expresses much love, and sincere thanks to, GOD my Father, JESUS CHRIST my Savior and the HOLY SPIRIT my Keeper, for being my strength and for making me who I am today.

To my mother, Sarah Hargrove, who has always been an inspiration to me, and has always taught me to keep GOD first in my life and to follow my dreams. Mother, I love you.

My girls, my wonderful sisters: Diane (Princess) Hargrove and Lisa Denise Seay. I will never be able to express my love and appreciation for working unyieldingly on this project with me.

My brothers, Earl Sr., Wallace Jr., and Danny Sr. Hargrove, for much love and support.

My other near and dear family members Lois, Sunny, Neoma (you will always be the first niece and my girl), Carlette (Um Hum!), E.J., Ashley, and my sweeties, Danny (D.J.), Daniel (Cope), Lasarah, and Dan (Lil' Wallace). No I did not forget you Eric, and my Louisiana Family (Momma Queen Ester Seay, I told you I would do it).

To the clergy that I ultimately respect, my pastor, Superintendent Clethen and first lady Susan Sutton, and Bishop Matthew and Mother Gayle Williams, and Elder Charles and Mother Delores Davis.

My first Pastors, the late Bishop W.E. Davis and the late Elder

Larry Mitchell Sr. Two great men of GOD that taught me a lot about living Holy.

To my prayer partners across the globe, Mother Hardge, Mother Rogers, Mother Starks, and the late Mother Annie Brown (that 4:30 prayer every morning is paying off). To Fran Harvey, Kaye Glen (your encouragement will never be forgotten. If I never told you that I appreciate you, I'm telling you now.), Bonnie Barnes, Angela King, Willetta Glen (surprise!), Jackquelyn Anderson (an awesome, powerful, and anointed prayer warrior), Evangelist Earlene Brinson, and all of you whose name I did not mention, but you know who you are. You are all special to me. I have too many friends, and associates to name one by one, but God knows I appreciate you all.

To my church families, Miracle Temple C.O.G.I.C., College Hill C.O.G.I.C, Browns Memorial C.O.G.I.C., Pentecostal Temple C.O.G.I.C., and all the C.O.G.I.C. family Internationally, thank you.

To all of the Churches who have opened their doors for me, to allow the Lord to use me, and share what He had to say through me.

To all of my Brothers and Sisters in CHRIST around the world, thank you.

In loving memories of my Father, Wallace Lee Hargrove, Senior (Pops), thanks for everything he has ever taught me. He will always be remembered. Father I miss you, but rest in peace.

Finally to all of the bookstores nationwide who will sell my book, and the hundreds of book clubs that will read and discuss the book, and especially to you the thousands of individual readers who will support this book, May GOD forever bless you and I am forever grateful. **"Love is what it Does."**

Printed in the United States
18593LVS00004B/58-306

9 781594 675638